The Church Alumni Association

The Church Alumni Association

A Handbook for Believers in Exile

Robert P. Vande Kappelle

WIPF & STOCK · Eugene, Oregon

THE CHURCH ALUMNI ASSOCIATION
A Handbook for Believers in Exile

Copyright © 2021 Robert P. Vande Kappelle. All rights reserved. Except for brief quotations in critical publications or reviews, no part of this book may be reproduced in any manner without prior written permission from the publisher. Write: Permissions, Wipf and Stock Publishers, 199 W. 8th Ave., Suite 3, Eugene, OR 97401.

Wipf & Stock
An Imprint of Wipf and Stock Publishers
199 W. 8th Ave., Suite 3
Eugene, OR 97401

www.wipfandstock.com

PAPERBACK ISBN: 978-1-6667-2577-3
HARDCOVER ISBN: 978-1-6667-2575-9
EBOOK ISBN: 978-1-6667-2576-6

08/04/21

Unless otherwise noted, Bible quotations are from the *New Revised Standard Version of the Bible*, copyright © 1989 by the Division of Christian Education of the National Council of the Churches of Christ in the United States of America. Used by permission.

I stand by the door.
I neither go too far in, nor stay too far out.
The door is the most important door in the world–
It is the door through which people walk when they find God.

. . .

There's no use my going way inside, and stay there.
When so many are still outside and they, as much as I,
Crave to know where the door is.
And all that so many ever find
Is only the wall where a door ought to be.

. . .

Sometimes I take a deeper look in.
Sometimes I venture in a little farther.
But my place seems closer to the opening.
So I stand by the door

. . .

I had rather be a door-keeper,
So I stand by the door.

—SAM SHOEMAKER

Contents

Preface | ix

1. Leaving Church | 1
2. Church in the Christian Tradition | 11
3. Worship in the Christian Tradition | 23
4. The Sources of Authority, Part I | 41
5. The Sources of Authority, Part II | 53
6. The Crisis of Authority in Modernity | 62
7. Postmodern Spirituality | 76
8. Rethinking Revelation | 94
9. Incarnational Theology: The Embodiment of Love | 115
10. "Healthy" Religion and "Junk" Religion | 132

Bibliography | 141
Index | 145

Preface

I have never not been in love with God. I can honestly say that my relationship with God has been dominant in my life, the driving force behind my thought and action. While the desire to love and please God is my highest priority in decision-making and the central factor in my choice of mate and career, this desire is also the most paradoxical and mystifying element in my consciousness, the perennial "thorn in my flesh."

Until recently, I attended church regularly, often as preacher and liturgical leader. However, in my retirement, I stopped going to church. Having once found church inspiring, animating, even liberating, I now find it static, pedantic, even constricting. Once a locus of revelation and truth, church now seems contrived, formulaic, and insular. What happened? I am not sure, but perhaps the best answer is that I have moved into a new level of faith, a stage I describe as Clarity in my book *Outgrowing Cultic Christianity*.

In the past, I believed loving God meant reading the Bible, attending church regularly, living ethically, and repenting of sin. Now, I love God by loving the world and other human beings, by appreciating the beauty around and within me, and by enjoying every moment of life as a gift of God's love for me and for all creation. That is more love than any one person can handle, and I don't wish to squander God's love by affirming doctrines or worshipping in ways that promote divisiveness and contribute to racism, sexism, nationalism, exclusivism, and other harmful attitudes or ideologies.

Whereas I once saw Christianity as the only true religion, and belief in God, the Bible, and Jesus as the sole way to heaven, I now view the Christian life as relational and transformational, as dynamic rather than passive, as life-affirming rather than life-denying. Being Christian is no longer about meeting requirements for a future reward in an afterlife, and not very much

Preface

about believing. Rather, for me the Christian life is about a relationship with God that transforms life in the present, that affirms religious pluralism, and that views faith relationally rather than dogmatically—as a way of the heart and not of the head.

While some Christians can experience this transformation in traditional church settings, I find such settings an impediment to this transformation. I need a new setting, a new understanding of the church, a new pattern for Christian living and thinking, a new vision. This book charts that vision.

1

Leaving Church

A YEAR OF COPING with coronavirus restrictions kept many people away from church. Pandemics and health crises, however, are not the only reasons people stop going to church. Many today have been swept up by the avalanche in America known simply as the "nones." They have decided, for one reason or another, to stop attending church, thereby joining the ranks of the religiously unaffiliated, dubbed the "church alumni association" or perhaps more accurately "believers in exile" by Anglican Bishop John Shelby Spong.

Church Alumni Association

Most of us associate the term "alumni association" with academics, particularly with secondary and post-secondary education. If you have a degree or diploma from high school or college, you automatically qualify. Once you have completed your education or training, you don't have to go back to school. You are done, and you are expected to move on in life. Of course, as an alum, you are encouraged to return to visit your alma mater, and usually a weekend, called "homecoming," is devoted to this celebratory tradition.

If you graduated from college, you can always enroll in a class or two, or even complete another degree or concentration, and graduate and postgraduate study are always available. In some cases, classes are offered for ongoing education, but once you received your degree or completed your training, you are a card-carrying member of the alumni association. As a responsible alum, you are encouraged to make regular financial contributions to support the ongoing work of the institution. If you wish to become more involved, you may be asked to join the alumni board and, if successful, even to be become a trustee of the institution.

Things are a bit different with church. You may move through the ranks of Sunday School and formally join the church as an adult member, but there is no degree to complete or diploma to receive. As a church member, you are expected to attend worship faithfully, to contribute financially, and to serve the mission of the church as you are able. If successful, you may be asked to teach a class or serve on a church board or in some other leadership capacity.

The goal, however, never includes joining the church alumni association, for such an organization does not exist. If you find yourself in that capacity, it is because you have stopped attending church, have attained nominal status as a "Christmas and Easter Christian," or are simply "shopping around," unaffiliated and uninvolved.

I recently spoke by phone with my friend Georgia. Her home church, a small Presbyterian congregation in rural Western Pennsylvania, had continued meeting during the coronavirus pandemic. The church's small size allowed congregants to maintain social distancing and other precautions that kept them safe during a period of high contagion. Since our conversation took place around Palm Sunday, I wished her a Happy Easter. We talked about going to church and she asked me whether I was attending. I told her that as a member of the clergy, I belonged to a presbytery, which prevented me from holding membership in a local church. Furthermore, since my retirement from presbytery, I only occasionally attend church, no longer needing its routine for discipline, growth, or worship. I believe I am dealing with these necessities in my daily practice of meditation, through my ongoing ministry as researcher and author of topics on spirituality, and through relationships with select friends and family, including my wife, also an ordained minister as well as a pastoral counselor.

Georgia responded by questioning her own worship experience, noting that she often found preaching limiting and even uninspiring. Her role as convener of study groups in her church includes inviting and welcoming attendees from other churches and of differing theological persuasions, and these discussions, ecumenical and heartfelt in nature, create in her theological perspectives and intellectual challenges frequently unmet in weekly Sunday worship. Despite regular church attendance, she too seems to be gravitating inexorably toward denominationally unaffiliated status.

Leaving Church

The Bad News: Declining Religious Affiliation

In her March 29, 2021 *Washington Post* article on church membership, religion reporter Sarah Pulliam Bailey declared that church membership[1] in the U.S. had fallen below 50 percent. This marked the first time church membership had fallen below the majority level since Gallup first asked the question in 1937, when church membership was 73 percent. During the first two decades of 2021, research data shows a seismic shift in the U.S. population away from religious institutions and toward disaffiliation.

Gallup's data find that church membership strongly correlates with age; whereas 66 percent of American adults born before 1946 belong to a church, this compares to 58 percent of baby boomers, 50 percent of Generation X, and 36 percent of millennials. While a significant percentage of Americans still attend church, they do not consider membership to be important, particularly those who attend nondenominational churches. However, no matter how researchers measure people's faith—whether by attendance, giving, or self-identification—Americans' attachment to institutional religion is in decline. According to political scientist Ryan Burge, also a pastor in the American Baptist Church and author of *The Nones: Where They Come From, Who They Are, and Where They Are Going*, by 2050 the United States will no longer have one dominant religion.

This trend, however, cannot be blamed on the coronavirus epidemic, which forced most places of worship to close in March, 2020. While the epidemic has disrupted public religious life, with most people unable to attend mass gatherings, polls conducted by the Pew Research Center indicate that rather than cause a decline in America's religiosity, Americans are more likely than their counterparts in other countries to state that their religious faith has been made stronger by the pandemic.

Experts attribute the national decline in religious affiliation to two major trends among younger Americans. First, to a broad shift suggesting a larger distrust of institutions in general. Some Americans are disillusioned by the behavior of religious leaders in general, including the Roman Catholic Church's sexual abuse scandal and strong White evangelical and Catholic alignment with former president Donald Trump. A second major trend is global support for mixing and matching elements in various religious traditions to create individualized faith systems. However, many people who do

---

1. Understood broadly, church membership includes members of churches, synagogues, and mosques.

not identify with a particular religious institution still say they believe in God, pray, read scripture, and follow other rituals that tend to be associated with religious faith. This is particularly true of younger generations that grew up with the Internet, a mechanism that provides new ways to relate to information, texts, and hierarchy. Internet culture celebrates ownership, promoting the idea that people can recreate personal narratives, having ownership over curating their own experience.

Interestingly, Shadi Hamid, a senior fellow at the Brookings Institute, argued in a March 10, 2021 essay for the *Atlantic Magazine* that what was once religious belief is being replaced by political belief. On the political right, Hamid stated, conservative Christians focused on Trump as a political savior, whereas on the political left, sin and salvation have been repurposed for secular ends. Lacking clear religious leadership or a transcendent source that defines belief or guarantees truth, morality, and social justice, Americans are appealing to other sources for goodness and well-being. Americans cannot live in a vacuum. However described, they are "believers" in some sense, and they require structures of belief and belonging. The question remains, "Can anything take the place of religious affiliation?"

The Good News: The Great Global Awakening

When we think about the history of religion in America, it is customary to speak of reform, revivals, and Awakenings, and to distinguish between three or possibly four Great Awakenings. The First Great Awakening (c. 1730–760) marked the end of European styles of church organization and created an experiential, democratic community of faith called evangelicalism. The Second Great Awakening (c. 1800–1830) ended Calvinist theological dominance and initiated new understandings of free will that resulted in a voluntary system for church membership and benevolence work. Historians have described this awakening as an Americanization of religion.

The Second Awakening led to the Social Gospel movement, with its progressive politics; the Pentecostal movement, with an emphasis on miraculous transformation; and nonconformist movements like the Jehovah's Witnesses, the Seventh-Day Adventists, and Christian Science.

During each Awakening, old patterns of religious life gave way to new ones, spawning new organizational forms that focused on revitalizing social, economic, and political life. Some writers say America is experiencing a Fourth Great Awakening (c. 1960–present), using terms such as postmodern, emerging (or emergent), and convergence to define it. Because this Awakening is affecting all religion in America, not just American Protestantism as in the past, it might be better described as the Fourth Great Awakenings (plural). The distinguished Harvard theologian Harvey Cox described this multireligious awakening as the Age of the Spirit, a widespread, experiential, practice-centered spiritual impulse sweeping across the globe. With such scope, it may not be the "Fourth" of anything, but rather the Great Global Awakening, the first of its kind. Whether the "age of belief" has ended, as Cox suggests, or the new has begun, as William McLoughlin proposed in his influential book *Revivals, Awakenings, and Reform* (1978), this latest Awakening, said to be occurring in the present, is long-lasting, in part because it is viewed to have unfolded in two distinctive periods (1960–980 and 1995–present), with an interlude in between.[2]

The first phase, unfolding during the 1960s and 1970s, was a time of dramatic change, characterized as progressive, countercultural, pluralistic, and antiauthoritarian. As a result, two forms of evangelical religion emerged in the 1970s and 1980s: (1) romantic evangelicalism, an experiential, internally driven faith, and (2) dogmatic evangelicalism, a belief-centered, externally driven faith. The first, inclusive by nature, embraced newness and change; the second, exclusive, authoritarian, and nativist by nature, focused on stability and conservatism.

What happened religiously during the interlude between these two phases is quite stunning, including an increase in the number of Americans who claimed no religious affiliation (the number nearly doubled between 1990 and 2009, rising from 8 to 15 percent). In addition, the percentage of self-identified Christians fell 10 points during this period, from 86 to 76 percent, while the percentage of people who claimed they were unaffiliated of any particular religion doubled, rising to 16 percent. Furthermore, during that period, the number of people who described themselves as atheist or agnostic increased almost fourfold, from 1 million to 3.6 million.

What characterized the first phase of this Fourth Awakening is that all sorts of people—even mature, faithful Christians—were finding conventional religion increasingly less satisfying. However, despite attending church less regularly, they longed for new expressions of spiritual community. McLoughlin characterized his Fourth Awakening as a "Romantic" awakening of experiential, quest-oriented, and self-aware religion. This emerging spirituality was grounded in a new social vision, for it included

---

2. Bass, *Christianity After Religion*, 241.

a profound commitment to justice, pluralism, freedom, and inclusive democracy. Other analysts dubbed this movement the "Next Christendom," claiming that America was witnessing the most significant change in the Christian faith since the Protestant Reformation. Traditional Christians watched from the sidelines, perplexed at the unfolding drama of this paradigm shift.

What characterizes the belief-driven second phase of this Fourth Awakening, particularly 2010 to the present, is a nativist religio-political movement that began with the strong backlash against President Obama known as the Tea Party. It was concretized and revitalized by President Trump under the slogan "Make America Great Again" (MAGA), a movement like the one described by William McLoughlin of reactionaries who look backward to a golden time, when the system worked; they insist that it will still work if only everyone confesses to the old standards.

Fear is still a powerful motivator, and the good old days seem good to those caught in a web of economic change, collapsing industries, and social insecurity. Many people in groups such as the Tea Party and the MAGA movement are devout believers in God, their families, and their country. Reactionary believers often support paths of authority and order in days that seem unhinged. To them, complete conformity to a singular interpretation of the Bible is the only way to happiness and salvation.

Yet coercion and fear are never compassionate. In the past, periods of intense social change and periods of intense religious encounters between different faiths often resulted in historical tragedies when fear-based religious groups gained political power. We live in a time of religious warfare, not just between different religions, but rather, in a dangerous time of intrareligious warfare, between those with differing versions of the same faith. During the Trump presidency, the nativists returned with fury. This version of religious and political hatred has been described by observers as the worst in American history since the Civil War. The current mood in our country does not bode well for the future. Theologian Harvey Cox calls it the fundamentalist rearguard action of those clinging to "belief-centered" faith, the fearful opposition to this global Age of the Spirit. According to Diana Bass, nativists of all sorts are doing their best to halt the spiritual awakening of romantic realism, bent on undoing the future it might create.[3] Ironically, the global spiritual awakenings of hope and possibility have

---

3. Bass, *Christianity After Religion*, 250.

created global nativist movements of fear and dread: fear of spiritual change but also of economic, political, and social change.

Distinguishing "Religious" and "Spiritual"

The concept of "awakenings" is controversial and much debated, due in part to its multifaceted nature; the difficulty distinguishing between religious change, reform, and awakening; and the inability to date these movements with precision. Focusing on current shifts in Christian belief and practice, we begin by distinguishing between the terms "religious" and "spiritual." What do these terms mean, and how are they distinct?

For much of Western history, the words meant roughly the same thing: how humans relate with God through rituals, practices, and communal worship. However, the popular meaning of the words diverged during the twentieth century. The word "spiritual" gradually came to be associated with the private realm of thought and experience, while the word "religious" came to be connected with the public realm of membership in religious institutions, participation in formal ritual, and adherence to official denominational doctrines. In general, "spirituality" came to take a positive and attractive meaning, as somehow more authentic, whereas "religious" took on a more negative connotation. In the mind of traditionalists, however, the term "spirituality" suggested something vague or vacuous, lacking substance and consistency. Spirituality, however, is neither vague nor meaningless. While it lacks precision, the word "spiritual" is both a critique of institutional religion and a longing for meaningful correction.

In recent studies, religious pollsters in a number of countries have begun asking people whether they consider themselves "spiritual but *not* religious . . . religious but *not* spiritual . . . religious *and* spiritual . . . or *not* spiritual and *not* religious." The most surprising result is to the first option. In the United States, 30 percent of adults selected this option. In Canada, 40 percent selected this choice, and in England, as many as 51 percent state they understand themselves in this way. In 2009, Princeton Survey Research Associates found that only 9 percent of Americans considered themselves "religious but not spiritual," while some 48 percent viewed themselves as "religious and spiritual." The World Values Survey, associated with the University of Michigan, found that in many developed nations, as high as 70 percent of the population self-defined as "generalized spirituality in contrast

The Church Alumni Association

to traditional religions."[4] As these polls demonstrate, the word "spiritual" is far more appealing in post-Christian societies than the term "religious."

In her seminars across the United States, Diana Bass discovered that only 6 percent of the attendees self-identify as "religious only," 20 percent say they are "spiritual but not religious," while 72 percent of those who claim affiliation with a religious denomination consider themselves "spiritual and religious."[5]

While most Americans see themselves as "being religious" and "being spiritual," this has not always been the case. As recently as 1999, Gallup polled Americans asking whether they considered themselves to be spiritual or religious. At that time, 54 percent of the respondents answered "religious only," while only 6 percent answered "both spiritual and religious." Only ten years later, a *Newsweek* poll showed 9 percent answering "religious only," while 48 percent answered "both spiritual and religious." In both cases, the figures for "spiritual only" (30 percent) and "neither spiritual nor religious" (9 percent) remained the same.

What accounts for the significant change in the first two categories? What caused such a drastic shift in self-designation? While any number of factors might account for the change, the key to this discontent is found in the ten short years between 2000 and 2010, a period dubbed the "horrible decade." During that period, religious affiliation plummeted across the breadth of Christian denominations, while interest in spirituality grew.

What happened in the United States during the first decade of the twenty-first century was not good for religion as a whole, not just for Christian congregations or denominations. In particular, five major events revealed the ugly side of organized religion, leading to a "participation crash" across the religious spectrum. Diana Bass lists these as follows:

1. 2001: The September 11 terrorist attacks (despite a month or two of increased church attendance following the attacks, suddenly, without much fanfare, people stopped going to church)
2. 2002: the Roman Catholic sex abuse scandal
3. 2003: Protestant conflict over homosexuality
4. 2004: The Religious Right wins the battle, but loses the war (while the second election of George W. Bush in 2004 proved to be a great

---

4. Bass, *Christianity After Religion*, 66.
5. Bass, *Christianity After Religion*, 92.

victory for conservative evangelical religion, it also alienated an entire generation of young people)

5. 2007: The Great Religious Recession (despite religious growth and optimism in the late 1990s, the early 2000s saw a significant drop in public trust in religious institutions. The economic recession of 2007 arrived at a moment when churches and denominations were in significant decline. The economic crisis did not drive people to religion; instead, it drove religion farther into irrelevance).[6]

By 2015, the phenomenon of shrinking faith communities was so widespread that "nones" (that is, the unaffiliated) became the third-largest religious identity in the world (16 percent), behind Christians (31 percent) and Muslims (23 percent), and just ahead of Hindus (15 percent).[7] And more Americans are joining the ranks of the religiously unaffiliated. Today there are more religious "nones" than Catholics or evangelicals, and 36 percent of those born after 1981 don't identify with any religion.

As it turns out, the current problem is not just a religious problem but also a human problem. In the absence of religion, fractious humans are simply uniting and dividing around other things: ideologies, dictators, demagogues, racial identities, wealth, weaponry, patriotism, conspiracy theories, revenge, and hate groups. If human beings don't consolidate and unite, antagonistic individuals and nations will sooner or later press the red button and nuclear weapos will fly. And they will quickly discover that radiation does not discriminate between Christian, Muslim, atheist, or humanist flesh. Whether the bombs fall in the name of God, race, nation, revenge, or economic ideology, there will be no winners when civilization self-destructs.

Less dramatic but no less catastrophic, ego- and money-driven individuals and corporations will keep plundering the earth, risking the long-term health of all life on earth for short-term returns for their corporate investors. Rising sea levels, hurricanes, wildfires, and droughts won't discriminate between black or white lives, Christian or Muslim lives, rich or poor lives, socialist or capitalist lives, even between "nones" and the religiously minded. None of this will matter to a destabilized ecosystem.

Ultimately, we need radical change in each sector of life, flowing from a new set of values and deeper spiritual narratives. And we need

---

6. Bass, *Christianity After Religion*, 76–83.
7. April 2, 2015 Pew forum; cited in McLaren, *Faith After Doubt*, 109.

The Church Alumni Association

forward-leaning faith communities to nourish those values and narratives in the context of a new kind of faith, a faith characterized by humility rather than arrogance, solidarity with the other rather than exclusion and antagonism, courage rather than fear, collaboration rather than competition, and love rather than self-interest.

Questions for Discussion and Reflection

1. In your own words, define the meaning of the phrase "church alumni association." Do you know anyone who joined recently? Are you a member? Explain your answer.

2. Assess the merits of Ryan Burge's prediction that by 2050 the United States will no longer have one dominant religion. In your estimation, will a new form of church emerge by then? Is such an emerging church already present and growing in the U.S., or will most believers simply fall into secular patterns of life and belief? Explain your answer.

3. How do you answer the question, "Can anything take the place of religious affiliation"?

4. Define the term "religious Awakening." How many Awakenings have scholars identified in America to date? When have they occurred, and what changes did they bring to society and to American Christianity?

5. Using Diana Bass's analysis, describe the difference between the terms "religious" and "spiritual." If you were asked to choose between them, which would you select? Why?

6. Describe the events that coalesced to shape the religious discontent that emerged in the U.S. between 2000 and 2010, accounting for the period known as the "horrible decade." If you were alive at the time, were you affected by these changes? Explain your answer.

2
―

Church in the Christian Tradition

RELIGION, WITH ITS SACRED times and places, embeds people into groups and congregations. Through rituals, routines, and periodic celebrations, individuals are provided a sense of belonging. This regularity, in turn, makes people more confident, hopeful, and productive. The book of Proverbs maintains that where there is no common vision, society perishes (29:18 KJV). Likewise, where there is no individual sense of purpose, human beings invariably fall short of their potential. In his attack on religion, *The Genealogy of Morals*, the atheist philosopher Friedrich Nietzsche (1844–1900) criticized modernity not only for ending traditional religion but also for fomenting nihilism. In its simplest sense, nihilism is a state in which one's life has no overarching good, no orientation or direction. Nietzsche claimed that for life to have meaning, human wills must have a goal. In his estimation, Christianity's goal (which he called "the ascetic ideal") and humanism's goal (which he called "the life-affirming ideal"), often clash, for while the former is based on rejecting this world for the bliss of eternity, the latter is based on acceptance of this world, with its temporal uncertainty, suffering, and pain but also its potential, goodness, and beauty.

In his assessment of Christianity, Nietzsche was partly correct but most certainly also misled, for the essence of Christianity is both life denying and life affirming. For Christians, church serves this dual purpose. Found in every city and in most towns and neighborhoods in the Western world, local churches provide believers opportunities for celebration, worship, fellowship, and instruction. Like its central symbol the cross, churches provide cohesion vertically and horizontally, binding people to God, the cosmos, and one another through love of neighbor and self.

The Church's Nature: Visible and Invisible

Any attempt to study Christian theories of the church begins with the origins of the community of faith, described in the Bible, as well as the emerging understandings of the nature and identity of that community. The church has always stressed its historical and theological continuity with the people of Israel. For this reason, we begin our exploration with the Old Testament, that is, the Hebrew scriptures.

If we are to understand the doctrine of the church, we need to become familiar with the biblical concept of corporate personality. The Bible portrays Israel as God's people, not simply a collection of persons but a divine company ("a priestly kingdom and a holy nation"; Exod 19:6; 1 Pet 2:9). Out of families, clans, and tribes God formed a nation, with a corporate personality: when one person suffered, everyone suffered; when one person was blessed, the people enjoyed the benefits; when one person sinned, the whole nation participated in the judgment; when one person received a promise, he or she did so on behalf of the nation.

Americans today live in an individualistic and pluralistic society, with diverse cultures, religions, and societal values. Ancient societies were quite the opposite; they were homogeneous, with little tolerance or diversity, and with no such thing as freedom of religion. The concept of corporate personality provided Israel with stability, solidarity, and unity during the period of its ascendency. These qualities enabled Israelites to maintain social and religious cohesion in a sea of paganism. Their laws, rituals, and values provided them with a distinctive way of life, which has preserved the Jewish people to this day. In order to be a community the Israelites needed land—physical and geographical space where they could carry out their theocratic uniqueness—and a temple—where they could make their pilgrimage, bring their tithes and offerings, and celebrate their festivals.

To understand the biblical concept of community, one must begin with Abraham. God started with one family, declaring a promise so wondrous yet absurd as to engender laughter, creating something in Sarah's womb when she was unable to conceive: "Is anything too wonderful for the Lord?" (Gen 18:14). From Isaac came Jacob, and from him the twelve tribes of Israel. They took his name, his personality, his style of life, and the covenant he had with God. They would call themselves "*bene* Israel," sons of Israel. The doctrine of election was not arbitrary. Rather it reminded them that they were beloved, God's intentional creation. They were not one nation *out of* many, but one nation *for* many. In such unity there is resolve, resilience, and strength.

In the Bible, the prototypical model for the community of faith is found in the patriarchal stories of Genesis 12–50, starting with the story of Abraham. It soon becomes evident that the underlying significance of chapters 12–50 is not the stories of the patriarchs but the story of Israel's self-understanding. At the time this material was put into writing, the main question was not, "Who are Abraham, Isaac, Jacob, and Joseph?" but "Who is Israel?" Israel was grappling with her identity, her self-understanding as a people called by God. The theological answer was found in the doctrine of election.

What does election mean? The biblical answer is given in the portrayal of Abraham, Isaac, and Jacob, patriarchs whose lives were characterized by the following traits:

1. They *lived by faith in God*. In Abraham, Israel understands something about herself, that she has been called into existence by God himself, that she has been created by God's initiative and preserved by God's grace. This would become a dominant theme during the Babylonian exile (see Isa 41:8–10).

2. They were *called to be a servant people*. Election does not mean that one people is chosen because they are better than others, but rather that they are called to spread God's grace. God's purpose is seen in Genesis 12:3 ("in you all the families of the earth shall be blessed"); it is a universal purpose, one that moves from particulars to universals, from individuals to communities and nations. In Abraham, God brings one person of faith into existence in order that God's blessing might be extended to all humanity. This is the Bible's stress on election, that when God calls a people, they are called to service, and the rest of the Old Testament, and then the gospels and epistles, show what it means to be a servant people. The Bible makes it clear that Israel's calling is part of God's healing intention (the biblical word for healing, health, wholeness, and goodness is "salvation," like the Hebrew word "shalom"). In the Bible, the election of a people becomes the basis for good news, what the New Testament calls "gospel." This

The Church Alumni Association

is the message of Genesis 12–50, and it is transported to a higher key in the New Testament.

3. They were *called to a life of pilgrimage*—a life of mobility, movement, and change. Biblical faith is a calling faith, a calling to go forth, to be on the way, to be moving in God's direction, to be pioneers of faith. Abraham was told to break his ties with his land and his former security, a way of life that up to that point had been deeply rooted to the land. Like Abraham, God's people are called to a nomadic consciousness. We see that so clearly in the prophetic consciousness, a stance that could be counter-cultural in the sense that one could be both an agent of change and a critic of the established order. The prophetic message was that God was doing a new thing. As we see in Abraham, faith is not so much consent or agreement as something dynamic, manifested in movement. So Abraham is the ancestor of a pilgrim people, as we learn in Hebrews 11, and his story highlights the themes of mobility and change, meaning that when faith becomes lifeless, stagnant, or frozen, whether into institutions with superiority complexes or into self-serving lifestyles, God breaks them down and forces his people into radical recommitment. The story of Abraham and the patriarchs is the story of God on the move with his people.

Historically and institutionally, the church emerged from the Jewish synagogue, following its threefold function as (1) a religious center, that is, as a place of worship and prayer, (2) as an educational center, that is, as a place of instruction and study, and (3) as a community center, that is, as a place where unique religious practices and traditions are maintained and festivals are celebrated.

The term "church" is not easy to define, for the institution it names is complex and multidimensional. For the sake of clarity, when we speak of the church, we envision four overlapping entities: (1) Christianity in general; (2) a visible ecclesiastical organization such as the Catholic, the Anglican, or the Lutheran Church; (3) a local congregation of believers; and (4) the invisible church (*kirk*) throughout the ages, an entity on earth sometimes called "the church militant" (as contrasted with "the church triumphant," a reference to departed brethren). While the term "militant" suggests antagonism between the church and the world, used ecclesiastically the word refers to the church on earth working to overcome defective dimensions of human existence.

This study introduces another subtlety, the possibility of a mystical body of believers, whether in the pre-Christian period or throughout the Christian era, embedded in particular ecclesiastical organizations yet not confined or defined by such membership. This notion of God's people as an invisible church is biblical and yet was generally unknown throughout church history until it became widely acknowledged in the Reformation and post-Reformation periods. For this understanding of "church" we may use the term "*kirk*," based on the Greek adjective *kuriakē*, "belonging to the Lord." This term, found in several northern European languages, is often associated with the Scottish Church.

Though the tension between these perspectives of the church runs throughout Christian history, the New Testament writers did not distinguish between them. After all, the ecclesiastical structure was in its infancy, and the biblical writers assumed that "card-carrying" Christians, while worshipping in a local congregation, also belonged to the larger "body of Christ." Like an iceberg, the church was strategically visible yet largely invisible.

The New Testament Church

Every verse of the New Testament presupposes the new people of God, a new community called the church. From the beginning, Christians were described as "the body of Christ," followers of Jesus who showed by their lifestyle that they were a part of the new order that Jesus had announced and that they believed had now arrived. Theologically, the church was a microcosm of the transformation that God's new order would bring for the whole world. To be in the church was to have a foretaste of life as God's new people. Socially, the church in the Roman empire was an alternative society, based not on selfishness, greed, and exploitation, but on the new freedom and fellowship that Jesus had announced: freedom to love God and to love and serve others (Mark 12:29–31). As the church expanded across the Mediterranean world, it was indeed a new society—a context in which people of diverse social, racial, and religious backgrounds were united in a new and radical friendship. Because they had been reconciled to God, they found themselves reconciled to each other.

Jesus conceived his mission to be that of calling the remnant of Israel—twelve disciples, corresponding to the twelve-tribe structure of Israel—to covenant faithfulness. And when the meaning of Jesus' life, death, and resurrection came upon these disciples with overwhelming power at the festival of Pentecost (Acts 2), a powerful movement emerged, rightly termed the Age of the Spirit. This small community became a dynamic and militant church, with a message that "turned the world upside down" (Acts 17:6) and a gospel that was carried enthusiastically to the ends of the earth. The Acts of the Apostles gives the story of the emerging church. The expansion was amazingly rapid. Within ten years of the death of Jesus, there were Christian communities throughout Palestine and Syria; in twenty years, across Asia Minor and into Greece; and in twenty-five years, in Rome.

While stressing the newness of the church, we must also keep in mind the relation of this community to the entire Old Testament heritage. In a sense, the church regarded itself as the "New Israel," for like ancient Israel, congregants had a special role in history. The Old Testament narrates how a people was formed to be the bearer of God's purpose in history and the instrument of God's saving work. Israel was not primarily a race or a nation but a covenant community created by God's action. Having delivered Israel from slavery in Egypt, God made them a covenant people. Through many tumultuous years, God educated and disciplined them in order that they might understand more deeply the meaning of their special role.

It was Second Isaiah who understood most profoundly Israel's place in God's worldwide purpose. According to this prophet, Israel was called to be a "light to the nations" (Isa 49:6) and a servant whose sufferings would benefit all humanity (Isa 49:3; 53:4–6, 11–12). However, in the intervening years, this expansive vision was obscured. The last two centuries before Jesus witnessed a resurgence of Jewish nationalism that led in time to wars with Rome. In 70 CE the Romans destroyed the temple, leveled Jerusalem, and removed the last vestiges of Jewish statehood.

Thus, in the fullness of time, God acted once again to reconstitute the community of Israel—no longer bound by ethnic or nationalistic limitations but open to all people, Jew and Gentile alike, on the basis of faith. The new community did not establish a clean break with the people of God whose life story is portrayed in the Old Testament. Rather, as Paul puts it in his important discussion in Romans 9–11, the community is a "remnant chosen by grace." It is, so to speak, a "wild olive shoot" grafted onto the olive tree (Israel); the "branch" (Gentile Christians) is supported by the roots that reach down deeply into God's choice of Israel and God's faithful dealings with this people (Rom 11:17–24).

Church in the Christian Tradition

Though the early church regarded itself as the true Israel, outwardly it differed little from the numerous synagogues that existed in Jerusalem. Like other members of the synagogues, its members took part in the regular worship of the temple (Luke 24:53; Acts 2:46; 3:1), observed the Jewish festivals, and in general kept the Mosaic law. Although some parallels can be drawn with the ancient Hebrew temple observances, the church in the New Testament was more similar to the Jewish synagogue (a learning center) than to the temple and its cultic activities. The first Christians, themselves Jews or proselytes to Judaism, modeled church worship after synagogue worship. This pattern included readings from scripture, prayer, preaching, and singing. The service closed with a distinctively Christian addition, the breaking of bread (the Lord's Supper or Eucharist), the central mystery at the heart of Christianity (see Acts 2:42). At first, homes of believers served as the places of worship; only later did Christians build church structures comparable to Jewish synagogues. The cross became the central cultic object, rather than the Ark of the Covenant or Torah scrolls. The cross served as a sign of Jesus' crucifixion and resurrection and symbolized the meaning of these events. The first day of the week (Sunday), which commemorated Jesus' resurrection, replaced the Jewish Sabbath as the primary cultic season. In addition to the regular activities of worship and education, which helped to unify the new Christian community, the basic cultic acts were baptism and the Lord's Supper.

Such worship and religious practices did not emerge without problems, however, and new leaders were required. Initially, the disciples of Jesus (the Twelve) became prominent leaders of the Jerusalem church, with a smaller number—consisting of Peter, John, and James "the Just"—exercising greater influence. A somewhat larger group, known as apostles, became the preeminent figures in the spread of Christianity. This group included the Twelve, but the total company of apostles was more numerous. What made a person an apostle was a personal commission by Jesus (the Greek word *apostolos* means "one sent"). Apostles were ambassadors of the risen Lord, understood to have extraordinary authority in the church.

In the world beyond Jerusalem, the church generally assumed the form of a synagogue, that is, a congregation. The Greek word for church (*ekklēsia*) means a group of people called together. It is one of the words used in the Septuagint to designate the assembly of the people of Israel. Because the Jews chose the word *synagogē* for their assemblies, it is quite likely that the first Christians deliberately, and to avoid confusion, rejected the term

The Church Alumni Association

adopted by the Jews and chose the other. Almost from the start, church congregations were governed by elders (Greek, *presbuteros*), one of whom was chief. With the passage of time, the office of chief elder evolved into that of bishop. Ephesians 4:11 lists prophets, evangelists, pastors, and teachers after apostles among the spiritually gifted leaders of the early church. Apostles stand first in 1 Corinthians 12:28, followed by prophets, teachers, miracle workers, healers, helpers, administrators, speakers in tongues, and interpreters. In keeping with the order of both lists, Paul assigned particular honor to the office of prophet (see 1 Cor 14:1–19). While the authority of the apostle was derived from a connection with Jesus, that of the church prophet was entirely charismatic. As the church developed, the authority of the apostles was passed from the apostles to the bishops through apostolic succession, an authority initially not concerned with the passing of power but of correct teaching. Over time the charismatic offices in the church waned, whereas apostolic authority was deemed irreplaceable.

As developed by Paul, the church presupposes a faith community that is the source of social unity. All life, whether politics, economics, education, or religion, stands under the covenant relation to God. Within that conception, Paul introduced four decisive aspects of biblical thinking on the church and its members:

- All members are indispensable.
- All members are different.
- All members are equal.
- All members are responsible.

Whether Christians meet together for worship or fellowship, all members are indispensable for all have something to contribute (see 1 Cor 14:26–33). As a result, Paul asserts that every Christian has a distinct *charism*, a ministry that is not restricted by either ordination or some other special experience, but that is given to all by the work of the Spirit in the lives of believers (1 Cor 12:7). The bottom line is this: every Christian ought to consider his or her spiritual gifts as a ministry of service to others. A church based on these principles will surely last.

While the first Christians acknowledged individual transformation, they would have viewed it corporately rather than in isolation. When God gave individuals a vision or called individuals to service, it was for the larger good. When Jesus spoke of the good shepherd leaving the fold for the sake of one lost sheep, he had the flock in mind. When Paul spoke of believers, he had the church, the "body of Christ," in mind. Though individuals are deeply beloved of God, they are members of a larger entity. Likewise, when Jesus tells his followers that they will do the works he does and even "greater works than these" (John 14:12), he had in mind not the deeds of individual disciples but the corporate endeavors of his followers.

Their origin as a "little flock," ongoing and expanding throughout history, would proliferate to a global religion of staggering size and pervasive presence whose faith, resulting in deeds of kindness and compassion, would literally "move" social and economic mountains (see Mark 11:23). Despite these accomplishments, Jesus reminds his disciples that they are to abide in him, the true vine, for individually and apart from him, they can do nothing (John 15:1–8). Only by following his example, propelled by his vision and empowered by his Spirit, would they fulfill their God-given destiny.

The letter to the Ephesians, written by a devoted admirer of Paul during the last two decades of the first century, is influenced by a dominant concern, namely, the unity of the church under the headship of Christ. The church at this time had become predominantly Gentile and was in danger of losing its sense of continuity with Israel. The author of Ephesians, desiring to underscore the larger history and tradition that defined Christianity, as well as the mystical unity of believers in Christ, portrays that oneness in three predominant images: the church is (1) the body of Christ (1:22–23), (2) the building or temple of God (2:20–22), and (3) the bride of Christ (5:23–32). The church's solidarity, Paul makes clear in Galatians 3:28, has social implications, namely, challenging racial, social, and sexual barriers. Because Christ is one, church members are united. Because Christ is one, church members are equal. Because Christ is one, church members are free to serve one another.

Worship and Community

To be honest, most of us are not Christians through chance or by conversion; most of us were born into Christian families and taken to church at an early age. Over time, many of us have consented to that faith tradition, affirming the religious choices made for us by our parents. Some of us still worship with the congregation of our birth, though most of us have moved

The Church Alumni Association

and joined new churches. Others, unfortunately, have left church altogether and have rarely looked back.

In my estimation, perhaps the single most important part of spiritual formation is to belong to a congregation that nourishes you even as it stretches you. Some of you may not be involved in a church and others may belong to one that leaves you dissatisfied or frustrated. If so, find a church that nurtures and deepens your Christian journey, that encourages worship with all of your being—body, mind, and spirit. Find one that worships a living Christ and a loving God. Of course, choosing a church is not primarily about feeling good, but church is meant to nourish us, not to make us angry or leave us bored. If your church worship is repetitive and unimaginative, if it feeds your mind but not your spirit, or if it is too noisy or judgmental, perhaps it is time to change.

The kind of Christian community that will nurture you depends upon your background and psychological temperament. Some Christians are nourished by sacramental and liturgical worship, some by more informed or contemporary worship, some by charismatic worship, others by great preaching or inspiring music, and still others by worship with lots of silence.

Authentic worship is profoundly subversive, for it affirms that God alone is the source of blessing, that God is Lord and the lords of this world are not. In worship we taste and see that the Lord is God. In worship we practice the presence of God, and we are nourished in mind and in spirit.

Being part of a Christian community provides a setting for Christian education. This matters for both children and adults. Unfortunately, many children (and even some adults) are taught to read scripture literally, in ways that they will later need to unlearn. In a time of pluralism, multiculturalism, and rapid change, children and adults need to learn in ways that make sense in the twenty-first century, and not simply pass on outmoded teachings and techniques. It is difficult to give one's heart to something that one's head rejects.

In all world religions, the most common method of religious practice is participating in religious rituals or symbolic acts. Most humans are sacramental beings. They live and move symbolically and sacramentally. However, there is a problem with religious ritual, the temptation to celebrate these rituals as ends in themselves without taking the next critical steps. The first is the importance of personal experience with God. Rituals are, after all, a means toward an end, and when that end is not kept in mind, the religious rites can easily become a form of idolatry. The answer to this dilemma, of course, is not to eliminate rituals, for human beings need to express their religious instincts in visible, audible, and other human ways. Rituals also allow us to express the indispensable communal dimension in worship. Because unselfish love is the essential element in religion, worship necessarily brings us closer to other people, and that needs to be celebrated by listening and singing together and by supporting one other in many different ways. On occasion, we need to be alone with God, but the fruit of that personal experience results in the second critical step, in our love and service toward others.

Authentic worship is profoundly transformative. To worship is to experience God, and to experience God is to love and serve others. Christian service involves two interrelated dimensions: love of God, manifested in worship, and love of neighbor, manifested in bringing joy to others and in addressing human need. Being part of a church creates opportunities for the collective practice of compassion and justice. These include caring for people within the church, outreach programs for people beyond the doors of the church, and advocacy of justice in our communities and in society at large.

The Church's Mission

For those interested in understanding how faith and practice interrelate, a good place to begin is the Sermon on the Mount, found in Matthew 5–7 (an abbreviated and revised version appears in Luke's Sermon on the Plain; 6:17–49). The sermon, which incorporates some of Jesus' best-known teachings, ends with the powerful injunction that hearing and doing belong together. Those who know and do are likened to those who build their life upon a strong foundation, whereas those who know but do not do are likened to those who build on a weak foundation

The mission of the church is to serve the world that God loves unconditionally. Like God, the church is to be faithful and inclusive. Its role is to transform unbelievers to believers, and believers into doers, enabling them to talk the talk and walk the walk—simultaneously.

This is a unique moment in our world. In the face of new opportunities and a rapidly changing world, our nation is seeking to determine its nature and role. Our society and its institutions are floundering, uncertain of their identity. New leadership is needed, with new vision and renewed resolve. To rediscover its role as the salt and light company, the church needs to undergo reformation yet again, leading by example. The church needs to inspire the youth of the world, attracting the best to church vocations and lay ministry. The world is waiting for such a church, and when it appears, many will join. Like the first believers, such a church will turn the world upside down. Transfomed by God and energized by the Spirit model rather than the monarchical model of God, together we can help make our country's motto—"One nation under God"—a reality. When that church arises, God's eschatological kingdom will be realized yet again. We are the ones the world is waiting for.

Questions for Discussion and Reflection

1. If you attended church as a child, what did you imagine church to be, an extension of school, a social gathering, a place to be with family and friends, holy ground, God's house, or something else?

2. How were you taught to behave in church? What reasons or explanations were you given for these expectations?

3. Describe the practical and theoretical distinction between the "visible" and "invisible" church. In what ways do these concepts influence your understanding of the church and your sense of religious belonging? Explain your answer.

4. What does this chapter say about corporate personality? What would you say to someone who tells you that they have no need of the church because they can be a Christian individually?

5. Does God exhibit national, racial, social, or sexual bias? If not, what about the doctrine of election? Does God favor some people, all people, or none? Support your answer.

6. When reading about the New Testament church, what aspect caught your attention? Explain your answer.

7. What is your favorite part of church ritual or worship? Why?

8. If the nature of Christianity has changed since its inception in a Jewish setting some two thousand years ago, what might the church look like a century from now?

9. Describe your understanding of the ideal church. Do you know of a church that meets these ideals? Why or why not?

3
—

Worship in the Christian Tradition

EVERYONE NEEDS AN IDENTITY. To be human is to be self-conscious, and self-consciousness requires identity. Individually, identity provides meaning and purpose, which engender confidence, vitality, health, and well-being. Corporately, identity provides social cohesion, stability, security, and productivity. Without identity, societies become restless, unproductive, uncooperative, even violent and self-destructive.

Perhaps the earliest Christian autobiography—surely the most introspective of all Christian expressions of self-consciousness—is the autobiography of Augustine of Hippo, written in the fourth century CE. Called *Confessions*, Augustine begins his reflections with a powerful statement of adoration: "You are great, O Lord, and highly to be praised; great is your power and your wisdom beyond measure. Humans, a small part of your creation, wish to praise you; human beings, bearing their mortality, carrying with them the evidence of their sin and proof that you resist the proud. Nevertheless, to praise you is the desire of humans, this small part of your creation. You motivate humanity to delight in praising you, because you have made us for yourself, and our heart is restless until it rests in you."

Here, at the start, Augustine outlines the human dilemma: our ultimate goal is to return to the God who created us, but we are thwarted in fulfilling this desire by our sin and pride. As Augustine sees it, the tragedy of the human condition stems from the fact that worship is an innate drive, as essential to life as breathing, but it is a dysfunctional and unfulfillable instinct; hence, we are destined for frustration.

The Church Alumni Association

In the monotheistic traditions of Judaism, Christianity, and Islam, worship has both a private and a public component. In the New Testament, three Greek words in particular can be translated as "worship." The most common word for worship in the New Testament is the verb *proskuneo*. Viewed as an act of worship or prostration, it consists of homage directed to the divine. However, in the New Testament, the word is rarely if ever used as a synonym for religious meetings or assemblies (the only exception may be 1 Cor 14:25). In its broadest sense, "worship" and *proskuneo* refer to reverence and honor, while they also include ritual acts of service like sacrificial offerings, praise, prayer, listening to teaching, and benevolence that accompany Christian assemblies. However, congregational assemblies are never referred to as "worship" in the Bible.

A second word for worship in the Bible is the noun *latreia*, often translated as "service" in the Bible (see Rom 12:1). The Greek term means more than a cultic act; it was used of work for hire, and in its spiritual sense, means "holy work," namely, what one does in service and worship of God. *Latreia* can mean formal worship, but it carries an emphasis on internal attitude and motivation rather than merit, reward, or external religious work.

A third word for worship in the Bible is the Greek noun *leitourgia*, from which comes our word "liturgy." While it can refer to public service (see Rom 15:16), the broader sense of the term is "non-cultic service or ministry," meaning contributing to the needs of others (see 2 Cor 9:12, Rom 15:27). It is also used of Jesus' priestly ministry in Hebrews 8:2, 6.

Christian worship is, of course, a group activity. In contrast to the religions of the East, the monotheistic traditions strongly emphasizes corporate worship. This is particular true for Christianity. When Christians meet together, they often sense a profound unity, something they call *koinonia*, a deep inward fellowship in the power of the Spirit. One reason worship is a spiritual discipline is because it is an ordered way of living that gathers the faithful together so that God can transform them. True worship, then, is less an individual act and more a lifestyle. William Temple, Archbishop of Canterbury, defined worship as comprising a vast array of spiritual practices, including confession, contemplation, meditation, invocation, and surrender: "To worship is to quicken the conscience by the holiness of God, to feed the mind with the truth of God, to purge the imagination by the beauty of God, to open the heart to the love of God, to devote the will to the purpose of God."

Worship in the Christian Tradition

Public worship is organized around certain seasons of the year, days of the week, and times of day. It is structured in specific events and detailed activities. In some cases, elaborate ceremony—known as ritual—forms the context for public worship. This does not mean, however, that all Christians are equally reliant on ritualized forms of worship. It is best to view ritual as a spectrum ranging from minimally structured worship to highly structured worship, from what is called "low church liturgy" to "high church liturgy."

In its broadest sense, however, worship is private, a matter of everyday life. For this reason, the prayers, deeds, and religious practices that make up the piety of believers are not limited to certain times of the day or days of the week. They are part of religious practice, which is the ongoing personal translation of faith into forms of devotion suited to the activities and responsibilities of a person's daily life.

Worship has been described as "an acting out of meanings." For monotheists, the aim is to communicate one's thoughts and feelings to God. Less obvious, but equally important, is that worship displays deeply held beliefs and attitudes about personal values and communal life. In short, worship is a performance, an acting out of meanings that individuals and communities embrace as valuable, as well as a context for the cultivation of spirituality. As the circumstances of personal and community life fluctuate, as new visions for the future emerge, and as fresh appraisals of the past are made, worship is altered. In representing the life of individuals and of religious communities, worship both sustains tradition and serves as a medium in which evolving self-understandings can be expressed.

For Augustine, as for his church, prayer and ritual were key to salvation. Central to the faith is its ritual life, for most Christian communities have defined and identified their religion most succinctly through their worship. While ritual is an expression of belief, enacting the worldview encapsulated in any religion's myths and symbols, ritual also has a pragmatic function, in that it expresses, confirms, and makes intelligible individual and communal beliefs. An ancient Latin axiom expressed this insight powerfully (*lex orandi, lex credendi*, meaning, how one prays is what one believes).

As a form of cognition, ritual constructs models of reality and paradigms of behavior. In other words, ritual seeks to define reality; it can be a means of imposing order on a seemingly disorderly, painful, and indifferent universe. Experts remind us that ritual is an attempt to turn the world as it is into the world as it should be, fusing the imagined and the real into a unified vision. As a process of social interaction, ritual can be the richest expression of the collective mentality of a society.

Experiencing God[1]

During my formative years, when I was formulating my Christian worldview, I learned that religion was essentially a one-way street: God took the initiative (that was called "revelation," which was found primarily in the Bible), and humans responded (that was called "worship"), individually (through prayer and Bible reading) and corporately (in church). Another form of response was through witness (called "evangelism") and service. Service meant performing deeds of kindness and compassion, as well as contributing financially to the church (called "tithes") and to other worthwhile causes (called "offerings").

While God's primary revelation occurred long ago, during biblical times, God could still speak to individuals today, through the Holy Spirit. Believers were encouraged to have daily devotions—that is, a time of Bible reading and prayer—because it was through such activities, in addition to church worship, that God might speak directly to us. During these times we might expect guidance for daily living and gain a clearer understanding of biblical teaching, but only as clarification of what had previously been recorded in scripture, for individual insight could never contradict inspired truth.

As I progressed in my faith, I often questioned why divine revelation was relegated to one specific historical period, and that several thousand years in the past, and why such revelation was limited initially to one geographical region (Israel) and to one ethnic group (Jews). Why didn't God speak decisively today? I wondered. Was God unable to do so, or were modern humans somehow less able to receive revelation than their ancient counterparts?

Eventually I came to realize that my thinking was wrong, that it was driven by faulty questioning. God had never stopped communicating with humanity, and modern human beings are still able to receive revelation from God. Eventually I came to realize what Austrian Roman Catholic apologist Friedrich von Hügel (1852–1925) emphasized persuasively in his writings,

---

1. The material in the remainder of this chapter is adapted from chapter 7 of my book, *Potter's Workshop*. While this material occupies a necessary place in our discussion, it is intended primarily for those unfamiliar with my earlier book.

that holistic religion is comprised of three elements in creative tension with each other. First, mature religion has a historical or institutional element, resulting in a religious tradition that has been refined through practice.[2] Secondly, it required a mystical or emotional element, a direct experience of God. Thirdly, mature religion requires an intellectual or scientific element, including the refinement developed by rationality and the capacity for critical, analytical thought.

If religious practice neglects intellectual and scientific scrutiny, it can become weighed down with superstitious accretions, outdated cultural patterns, and self-serving ethical practices. Powerless to engage fully with the values and mindset of the generation in which it lives, such religion will lack the ability to express to others its truth in viable terms.

However, if religious practice seeks to eliminate the mystical and emotional element in favor of some rigid intellectual or ethical system or in an effort to preserve intact some set of traditional institutional forms, it will remain as useless as a furnace cut off from its electrical source.

My theological upbringing, I realized, was like a one-legged stool, unstable and unreliable, because it emphasized the institutional dimension, harnessing the intellectual and the mystical elements so directly to tradition that creative thinking and genuine experience of God became practically impossible. I discovered that my devotional practice, including church worship, was driven mostly by duty and obligation and far less by love and affection. My relationship with God had been stunted, not by lack of effort but rather by misguided effort.

Instead of disclosing what God has already revealed to the world, and that in singular and orthodox fashion (that is, through dogma and creeds), what if we viewed the central purpose of religion as discovering how humans can relate to God? Wouldn't that task require a variety of approaches? As God cannot be confined to a single image or understanding, neither can human experience of God be one-dimensional. If contact with God is possible, then communication on many levels becomes essential. Every human being has a unique personality structure, and this uniqueness becomes important as a possible avenue to God. The New Testament expression of this is seen in the description of the church as the "body of Christ"—a unified organism that embraces incredible diversity; indeed, that depends upon diversity for its existence.

---

2. For von Hügel, religious tradition determines and defines patterns of worship, scripture, and orthodox belief.

The Church Alumni Association

As individuals realize that they have their own unique way of interacting with the world, they will not attempt to force others into their mold. There is a place for each personality in the spiritual journey, a place for the religious thinker, the religious activist, the devotional practitioner, and the religious artist. There are many different ways of living the religious life and of experiencing God, each with its values, difficulties, and rewards.

How we conceive God determines how we experience God. Is God personal? The Christian tradition, as most religions, views God thus, with personal characteristics. Supernatural theism is unambiguously anthropomorphic. The natural language of meditation, devotion, and corporate worship is personal; we use this language regularly in our private devotional life and when we worship in church. There is nothing wrong with personifying God and addressing God as if God were a person.

Problems arise, however, when we literalize these personifications, as though "the right hand of God" means that God really has hands, and when God is said to speak, that God must have a larynx. Some years ago, a group of Baptists left the Texas Baptist Convention because they believed that God is male rather than female or sexless. Did they believe, I wonder, that God has male sex organs? If so, does God have to shave? Of course, such questions seem trivial, but they are not unimportant.

Perhaps we can ease some of the difficulty by a softer literalization of personal language for God, namely, by affirming that God is personlike. This means that God is separate from the universe, a living being separate from other beings and yet somewhat like us, though to a superlative degree. Nevertheless, literalizing these personifications leads to supernatural theism and the problems associated with it, such as the apparent contradiction between God's omnipotence, justice, and omnibenevolence. Human experience of God suggests that God cannot simultaneously be all-powerful, all-good, and all-loving, else there would be less injustice and tragedy in this world and more goodness and morality. Likewise, the biblical view of God can be an impediment to belief, for this God seems to display unattractive and even immoral behavior, displayed through qualities such as destructive anger, jealousy, and biased treatment of human beings. This God is depicted as choosing people selectively, fighting wars, defeating enemies, sending storms, plagues, and even death. Yet this God also heals the sick, spares the dying, and rewards goodness. Even normal human judgment condemns such behavior as inconsistent and immoral. In his publication *The Sins of Scripture*, Bishop Spong examines biblical moral principles attributed to the will of God and concludes that those who wish to base their morality literally on the Bible have either not read it or not understood it.

There are clearly problems associated with anthropomorphic personifications of God. Whatever God is ultimately like, whether personal, impersonal, or transpersonal (that is, more than personal), there are at least three dimensions of meaning to personal language of God that we need to retain:

- God's relationship to us is personal. It is doubtful that humans could worship something that does not have at least the status of personality.
- God has more the quality of "presence" than of nonpersonal "energy" or "force." To use language coined by the Jewish philosopher Martin Buber, God has the quality of a "Thou" rather than that of an "It," hence more the quality of a person than of an impersonal "source."
- God communicates with us, not necessarily audibly or by divine dictation, but God "speaks," sometimes through visions and dreams but also through "prodding" or "hunches." Vehicles for these can include other people, devotional practices, the scriptures of one's religious tradition, and daily circumstances.

As contemporary author Frederick Buechner advises, "Listen to your life. Listen to what happens to you because it is through what happens to you that God speaks." Paula D'Arcy states this truth more bluntly: "God comes to you disguised as your life."

Friederich von Hügel, valued more highly in his day as a spiritual director than as a theologian, found practical outlets for his significant intellectual skills. At the age of eighteen, sickened with typhus fever and left practically deaf, he embarked on a theological career. While he spent most of his life as a Catholic layman dedicated to theological and philosophical writing, at the age of forty he met the Abbé Huvelin, a distinguished spiritual director serving in a Parisian parish. Through his influence, von Hügel experienced a profound spiritual transformation that led him from his intellectual pursuits into the field of spiritual counseling, and it was as a guide and counselor that he made his greatest contribution.

Because of his deafness, much of his counsel occurred by correspondence, through the mail. Many of his letters exist in published form. Among those who sought his direction was Evelyn Underhill, distinguished in intellectual circles for her books on mysticism. Having the experience of a growing number of people who wrote to her for spiritual advice, she turned to von Hügel for help with her own spiritual formation. Because of her commitment to the mystical, experiential element in religion, she sensed an aversion to the institutional side of religion, particularly its historical and sacramental elements. Displaying a theocentric approach in prayer and worship, she belittled those who spoke of a relationship with Jesus or Christ, considering such attachment sentimental and unreal.

Sensing in her a tendency to go to extremes, either overemphasizing mystical (non-institutional) practices or their opposite, traditional (institutional) practices, von Hügel recommended moderation. Knowing "these two extremes to be twin sisters in such a soul as yours," he recommended the following minimal institutional plan: attendance at one church service on Sunday, with perhaps a midweek prayer meeting and one church-related retreat a year, coupled with a maximum of half an hour a day for private prayer and a three-to-five-minute examination of conscience at night before retiring. He also recommended the cultivation of some non-religious interest such as painting, music, or gardening, in addition to devoting two afternoons each week to visit the poor. This final option, he tells Professor Underhill, will do more than all the rest to blunt her intellectual religious bent and open her heart to the needs of all, and not only the audience of fellow intellectuals to whom her career had thus far been devoted.

More important than this, however, were von Hügel's efforts to get her to face the neglected side of the incarnational aspect in her religious life—of who Jesus Christ was and of what he revealed about God—making Christ's incarnation central to her thought and practice. From her writings, he knew she had a deep respect for Jesus, but this did not seem to carry through into her interpretation of Christianity or into her prayer life.

As a spiritual director, it was clear to von Hügel that there should be no coercion in the spiritual life. Dealing with a strong intellect, he believed that if his client did not face the neglected issue of the incarnation, there would be no spiritual growth. In her writings, she spoke often of what was mystical and symbolic in Christianity, but if she was to progress spiritually, she needed to become convinced, not of what ought to be real but of what in fact was historically real. Knowing her area of neglect, von Hügel asked her to consider changing her non-historical stance by acknowledging God's self-disclosure in Jesus Christ. If she could accept that much, not cognitively, by understanding it rationally, but by faith, then she could postpone decision

Worship in the Christian Tradition

concerning equally difficult yet ultimately less important items of belief such as the Virgin Birth and the Resurrection.

Regarding her prayers, he proposed no sudden change in her theocentric approach, but asked whether she might at least admit that praying through Jesus Christ was a possibility. Perhaps she might admit that her way of praying, apophatically[3] and to the Father alone, was one way but not the only way to pray. Could she continue praying as she felt led, yet introduce kataphatic images such as the Sea of Galilee and Calvary into her imagination? Such visualization might provide more credence to her understanding of the historical aspects of the incarnation. Such meditative prayer might also impact her understanding of God, help alleviate her doubt concerning the historical validity of Christianity, and increase her appreciation of God's presence in everyday life. It might also make her prayer more intercessory—more about others and their needs rather than exclusively about herself and her spiritual condition. Von Hügel's method served to draw her quietly yet progressively from her own self-sufficient efforts and merit to God's redemptive action through Christ, for only thus would she experience the transformation she desired.

After years of such direction, a new orientation emerged in Evelyn Underhill's life and writing. She did not convert to Catholicism, as some of von Hügel's directees did, but was drawn more deeply into her own Anglican tradition. Of von Hügel's advice she wrote: "I owe him my whole spiritual life, and there would have been more of it than there is, if I had been more courageous and stern with myself, and followed his direction more thoroughly . . . Until about five years ago, I never had any personal experience of Christ as Lord. I didn't know what it meant . . . Somehow by his prayers and advice, he compelled me to experience Christ . . . It took about four months—it was like watching the sun rise very slowly—and then suddenly one knew what it was."[4]

---

3. Apophatic worship is direct and not mediated. It comes from the Greek word meaning "without images." This mystical approach to the divine is based on the idea that one can best relate to the divine directly, apart from images and content. It emphasizes silence, emptiness, and self-renunciation. Kataphatic worship, by contrast, is indirect and mediated. It comes from the Greek word meaning "with images." In this approach, the divine is mediated through words, images, pictures, symbols, and rituals. This sensate or sacramental approach exemplifies much corporate worship.

4. Steere, *Spiritual Counsel and Letters of von Hügel*, 21.

The Church Alumni Association
Devotional Practice[5]

Christians speak regularly of God's love for humanity, but rarely about the importance of loving God. What does it mean to love God? Most of us are familiar with the biblical injunction to love God with all our heart, soul, mind, and strength (Mark 12:30). It has been called the "greatest commandment." But what does it mean? Simply put, loving God means paying attention to God and to what God loves. It means "practice"—practicing the presence of God.

Modern Western Christians, particularly Protestants, have not made practice central. Other Christians, Roman Catholics and Eastern Orthodox, emphasize rituals and practice. So also Jews, especially Orthodox Jews, who pay great attention to the "way of Torah." Likewise, at the center of Buddhism lies the "eightfold path," centered on practice. Muslims carefully observe the "five pillars" of Islam, four of which are about practice. One pillar requires praying five times a day, a practice that takes about forty minutes. How different might Christians be if they spent forty minutes a day in prayer and meditation. Forty minutes of prayer a day can transform a person's life!

A major reason that Protestants pay little attention to traditional Christian practice goes back to the Reformation, which contrasted "faith" and "works." Protestants are "saved" by faith, not by works. To many Protestants "practice" sound like "works." But the point of practice is not to earn salvation by accumulating merit. Rather, practice is about paying attention to God. Practice is how we love God.

The notion that God can be known (or experienced) is foreign in the modern world and in much of modern theology. In skeptical theology, the reality of God or the sense of God's presence has been replaced by emphasis on ethics, that is, on behavior. Modern Christianity largely downplays mystical and relational notions of God, emphasizing instead the importance of "being kind" or "being good." In liberal theology, the highest virtue becomes a passion for justice. However, Christian practice historically has been about our relationship to both God and neighbor, about both God and the world, and not about choosing one over the other.

An encouraging sign of renewal in the church is the recovery of practice as central to the Christian life. If the Christian life is about relationship and transformation, practice will be central. By practice I mean all

---

5. The material in this segment is taken from my book, *Potter's Workshop*, 82–91.

the things that Christians do together and individually as a way of paying attention to God. These include being part of a Christian community and taking an active part in its life, its worship, Christian formation, fellowship, and collective deeds of hospitality and compassion. In addition, they include devotional discipline, especially prayer and Bible study. Loving God also includes loving what God loves through the practice of compassion and justice in the world.

Like all relationships, life with God grows and deepens to the extent that we give it attention. It involves spending time in it, giving it thoughtful priority, and, ideally, enjoying it. Paying attention to our relationship with God matters because humans are ultimately relational. We don't first become ourselves and then have relationships. Rather, we are constituted by our relationships; they shape and form us. Likewise, paying attention to our relationship with God will shape us.

While many Christians enter Christianity through "conversion," they generally do not convert from another religion or from no religion at all. Rather, at some point they commit to a Christian way of life. Christian practice, essential to this process, transforms the deepest level of their being—the heart—and helps shape their Christian identity. The process of Christian identity and character formation leads from a limited identity to a larger identity, from a limited self to a larger self. This takes place through life "in Christ," and practice is how this happens. The Spirit of God works through practice. Practice is not simply something Christians do. Rather, practice nourishes them. This happens in corporate practice such as worship as well as through individual devotional practices. Christians are fed by practice.

Verbal Prayer

Like other spiritual practices, prayer is primarily about paying attention to God. There are three major types of Christian prayer: verbal prayer, meditation, and contemplation. Verbal prayer addresses God with words, whether audibly or silently, whereas meditation and contemplation are not about talking to God, but rather, listening for God.

There are five categories of verbal prayer: adoration or praise, thanksgiving, confession, intercession, and petition. The most common form of prayer, intercession and petition, focus on asking for something for ourselves or for others. This "wish list" approach requires an almost magical view of God—that God is an interventionist who sometimes answers prayer. Such a view of God is essentially untenable, for it presents insuperable problems.

For example, if God could have intervened to stop the Holocaust but chose not to, what kind of God would that be? Does it make any sense to think that God can intervene to stop terrorist attacks, or tornados from striking, or keep airplanes from crashing, but chooses (at least in some cases) not to? If so, why some and not others? And what about all the illness and tragedy that strike faithful believers? To suppose that God intervenes implies that God does so for some, but not for others.

Not only is the interventionist idea difficult in itself, but this idea of unanswered prayer is also problematic. Think of all the people who pray for safety and peace in time of war, or of those who pray for healing, and whose prayers are not answered. Yet we continue to pray in this fashion, and it seems right to do so, when it is practiced sincerely and maturely. For one thing, petitionary and intercessory prayer feel natural; they seem like a form of caring. In addition, we don't really know how prayer works. As we learn from physicians, prayers for the healing of others sometimes have unexplainable results, and perhaps other kinds of prayers do as well. While some healing might be psychosomatic—body and mind seem to be related in ways we do not fully comprehend—putting things in God's hands is beneficial. There is also the placebo effect. Trust increases expectation and reduces stress, both preconditions for healing and wholeness.

Regardless of their efficacy, petition and intercession, like adoration, thanksgiving, and confession, serve the central purpose of prayer. As previously noted, the goal of all prayer, including of meditation and contemplation, is intimacy. God isn't a vain emperor in need of worship and praise, nor does God need encouragement or sideline cheerleading. Even confession need not be demeaning or self-deprecating, in the sense of "I am so bad," or "here's where I have fallen short." Prayer is ultimately relational, about companionship. Even confession, when it is practiced, ought to be natural, like sharing thoughts about the day or concerns and desires for oneself and others with an intimate confidant.

Of course we might discuss prayer by thinking the obvious, namely, that God already knows about my day, but that misses the point. Our human nature is to share, for sharing is part of all intimate relationships. Our relationship with God deepens through disclosure and conversation. Like adoration, ultimately all prayer is a human way to love God.

Meditation

The second and third categories of Christian prayer are meditation and contemplation. While meditation is in vogue today, there is a difference between psychological relaxation techniques, Eastern meditational practices, and Christian approaches. Until recently, the Christian practice of meditation and contemplation occurred primarily in religious orders. Now they are being recovered by laity and clergy, Protestant and Catholic alike. What these practices have in common is that they do not involve talking to God, but rather listening for God. And they do so in different ways.

In recent years mind and brain science has discovered a greater understanding of the way our bodies and minds relate to each other. Meditation has been found to produce profound and largely positive effects upon both body and brain. As biofeedback training reveals, even average people can learn to control bodily functions that were once considered beyond conscious control.

In addition, meditational practice is known to produce remarkable psychological and physiological effects, bringing practitioners to deeper levels of brain functioning and to increased psychic awareness. Meditation and contemplation are known to produce alpha and sometimes theta waves, and in both of these states practitioners become more alert and perceptual ability may increase as the capacity of the mind changes. Physical reactions like blood pressure and heart rate, influenced by the mind, also become slower and steadier.

Meditation, a kataphatic approach to prayer, involves reflecting on an image, symbol, or phrase, sitting with it, holding it, remaining with it. A classic example is "Ignatian meditation," named after Ignatius of Loyola, the founder of the Jesuit order in the sixteenth century. This approach provides a structure for meditation on images in a biblical text. As we enter the text, the images of the text become means for God's Spirit to speak to us. Loyola's approach, recorded in his *Spiritual Exercises*, became the basis of the "Ignatian Retreat," a twenty-eight-day meditational retreat on the mission, life, passion, and resurrection of Jesus. By meditating on Christ's life and teachings, primarily through visualization exercises, participants are encouraged to become companions of the earthly Jesus, hence true and committed disciples of Christ.

In his *Study Guide for Celebration of Discipline*, Richard Foster provides a meditation on John 6—Jesus' feeding of the five thousand—that illustrates Loyola's meditational technique on scripture.[6] What follows is a paraphrase. Read the passage slowly, attempting to use all of your senses. Try to place yourself in the actual scene. Imagine yourself as the child who gives Jesus his lunch, or perhaps as one of the child's parents. Try to see the story—the hills, the faces of the people gathered about. Try to hear the story—the sound of the water, the noise of the children, the voice of Jesus. Try to feel the story—the hardness of the ground, the texture of your clothing. Finally, try to feel with your emotions—hesitancy at bringing your lunch, astonishment at the miracle of the multiplied food.

Then, in your imagination, watch the crowd leave and Jesus go up the hill. You are left alone. You sit on a rock and re-experience the events of the day. After a while, Jesus returns and sits on a nearby rock. For a time you are both quiet, looking out at the water and enjoying one another's presence. After a while, Jesus turns to you and asks, "What may I do for you?" Then you tell him what is in your heart, your needs, your fears, your hopes. When you have finished, you become quiet for a while. Then you turn to the Lord and ask, "What may I do for you?" And you listen quietly, prayerfully. No instructions are necessary, for you are just glad to be in Christ's presence. If words come, take them to heart. Often they will include practical instruction about some matter of life, for God wants us to live out our spirituality in the ordinary events of our days.

Contemplation

Contemplation is a form of prayer based on internal silence. The purpose of contemplation is to sit silently in the presence of God. Many churches offer training in contemplative prayer, and in some areas one can find workshops on it.

As with meditation, find a quiet place, removed from any distractions, and initiate what will become for you a daily practice of sitting in silence (you can start with a span of two or three minutes, though eventually you will want to build to two sessions of twenty minutes each) to simply become aware of God's presence in your life. According to experts in stress reduction and pain management, two twenty-minute sessions of structured relaxation a day, utilizing activities such as meditation, deep breathing, yoga, or tai chi, can be as beneficial in reducing stress and restoring wellbeing as

---

6. Foster, *Study Guide for Celebration of Discipline*, 20.

a two-hour nap. As it turns out, spiritual meditation achieves physical and emotional benefits while producing transformative spiritual results as well!

One of the most common forms of contemplation is called "centering prayer," associated especially with the Benedictine monk Thomas Keating. Through silence, the goal is to open your mind, and therefore your heart and entire being, to God. The goal is not to experience God directly, for as Keating reminds us, "God as He is in Himself cannot be experienced empirically, conceptually, or spiritually. [God] is beyond experiences of any kind. This does not mean that [God] is not *in* sacred experiences, but that God *transcends* them."[7] Nevertheless, sacred experiences lead us to the experience of emptiness, and the more one lets go, the stronger the presence of God becomes. Keating, one of Christianity's most reliable guides to meditation, put things into proper perspective when he cautioned that though all human beings are summoned into the presence of God by the fact of their birth, they become present to God only by their consent. "As our faculties and capacities to relate gradually develop and unfold," he noted, "the capacity to enter into new relationship with God increases, and each new depth of presence requires new consent. Each new awakening to God changes our relationship to ourselves and to everyone else. Growth in faith is growth in the right perception of reality."[8]

To get started, the following guidelines are indispensable. Begin by sitting comfortably, with your eyes closed. Sit in a straight chair, with your back erect and both feet flat on the floor. Rest your hands on your knees or thighs, palms up or down, whichever you find most comfortable. To calm yourself, take a deep, cleansing breath. Select a word or phrase that you will use throughout the period of silence; some possibilities include the words "joy, peace, love, grace, wisdom, unity, surrender, Christ, or Holy Spirit." It is helpful to choose a word or phrase that signifies your intent to consent to God's presence and action within. Of course, the sacred word you select is sacred not because of its meaning but because of its intent. It expresses your intent to consent to God, the Ultimate Mystery who dwells within you. Once you find a word or phrase you are comfortable with, try to stick with it. You may change words if you wish, but to avoid distraction, refrain from shopping around during the same period of prayer.

Sue Monk Kidd, a contemporary novelist, describes how this works. Having read *The Way of the Pilgrim*, the account of an anonymous Russian

7. Keating, *Open Mind, Open Heart*, 17.
8. Keating, *Intimacy with God*, §1.

peasant in the nineteenth century who sought to pray the ancient "Jesus Prayer" ("Lord Jesus Christ, have mercy upon me") all day long, she decided to use this as her centering prayer. She said it once, and then again, blending the prayer with her breathing as the pilgrim had done: "Lord Jesus Christ" on the in-breath, and "have mercy on me" on the out-breath. She repeated the prayer slowly, silently finding a rhythm that seemed to slow everything down, and this led her naturally to focus on Christ. As my centering prayer, I prefer to use phrases from the Lord's Prayer: "Thy kingdom come" on the in-breath, and "thy will be done" on the out-breath.

Because this time is dedicated to listening and reframing, Centering Prayer is not the time to pray consciously for others or for yourself. By consenting to God, you are embracing the past, present, and future, and the whole of creation. If you find a visual symbol to be more helpful than a verbal word or phrase, use it instead, but not as an object of meditation. Its sole use is to return you to silence whenever a conscious thought arises.

Another way to focus is to concentrate on your breathing, buoyed by its calming and rhythmic nature. As you do, taking slow, deep breaths, you will find it reducing stress and expelling other negative emotions lurking deep within. When thoughts intrude, gently return to your sacred word and focus on your breathing. As you practice regularly, the strength of habit will make it easier to let go of the normal flow of thoughts and distractions.

In our psyche there are obstacles to opening ourselves to God. As we quiet the mind, we discover various kind of thoughts arising from the stream of consciousness within. Some of these thoughts might be superficial, others insightful, and some may have emotional content. Some come from the unconscious, and may represent the consequences of traumatic emotional experiences stored in our bodies in the form of tension, anxiety, and various defense mechanisms. Ordinary rest and sleep do not get rid of them. But in interior silence and the profound rest that this brings to the entire organism, these emotional blocks begin to soften up, activating the natural capacity of the human organism to release things that are harmful. The psyche as well as the body expels material that is harmful to its health. When the unloading of the unconscious begins, many people feel that they are going backwards. If this happens, simply accept the emotion and continue the process. The practice will eventually bring about the necessary change of consciousness. Contemplative prayer is part of the whole process of integration, which requires opening to God at the level of the unconscious. Contemplation releases a dynamic that can be peaceful at times and at other times heavily laden with thoughts and emotion. Both experiences are part of the same process of integration and healing. Both are necessary to complete the process of transformation.

The goal of our practice is not contemplative prayer but the contemplative state, the permanent and abiding awareness of God that comes through the mysterious restructuring of consciousness. There will always be distractions in contemplative prayer. However, contemplative prayer is not on the level of thinking. It is consenting to God's presence in pure faith. Hence, the proper response to extraneous thought is to let it go. As Keating notes, "Do not resist any thought, do not hang on to any thought, do not react emotionally to any thought."[9]

Centering Prayer is not a duty and its goal is not proficiency. It is an exercise of intent, the cultivation of our will and our faculty of choice. During this time, our only activity consists in maintaining our intention to consent to God's presence and action. The ongoing journey then becomes whatever God wants it to be. If you are tempted to think that "doing nothing" for a period is invaluable, recall that no one hesitates to sleep at night. Practicing this prayer, however, whether in its abbreviated or lengthier version, is not doing nothing. It is a gentle form of activity, as long as the will keeps consenting to God. Returning to the sacred word or the act of breathing is enough activity to keep one awake and alert.

At the end of the chosen time span, slowly return to your ordinary world and thoughts. This may be a good time to converse with God or to refocus your thoughts. Take a minute or two before opening your eyes, because doing so suddenly can be uncomfortable. As your sensitivity to the spiritual dimension within develops with regular practice, you may begin to notice a heightened awareness of God's presence arising at times of ordinary activity. Keating likens this experience to the color added to a black-and-white television screen. The picture remains the same, but it is greatly enhanced. The color was present all along, but it was not transmitted because the proper receptive apparatus was missing. Centering Prayer is a way of tuning in to a level of reality that is always present and in which we are always invited to participate.

The sense of presence established during Centering Prayer has to be integrated with the rest of reality. If our method is effective, the presence of God becomes a kind of fourth dimension. It does not replace our three-dimensional world, but it becomes the most important dimension, that from

---

9. Keating, *Open Mind, Open Heart*, 99.

which everything emerges and to which everything returns. The contemplative state is established when the circumstances of our life move from being experiences in themselves to an abiding state of consciousness.

Daily practice is essential for both Christian formation and nourishment. A famous passage from the prophet Micah offers a compact expression of biblical faith. Micah asks, "What does the Lord require of you?" His answer: "To do justice, to love kindness, and to walk humbly with your God" (Mic 6:8). Christian practice is about walking with God, becoming kind, and doing justice. It is not primarily about believing certain things about God or about being a good person. Rather, it is about how one become a good person through the practice of loving God.

Questions for Discussion and Reflection

1. In a sentence or two, express what worship means to you.
2. In the past, what role did public worship play in shaping your identity? Your values? Your beliefs?
3. Describe your current worship experience. Is it mainly public, mainly private, a combination of both, or nonexistent? If you answered "nonexistent," describe a scenario where you would find worship relevant, beneficial, and attractive.
4. How important is fellowship—the sense of belonging—in your church attendance and in your church selection? If you attend public worship regularly, name the top three reasons why you attend that church or place of worship.
5. In choosing a place to worship publically, how important is denominational affiliation to you? How important is the church's theological and traditional stance, whether conservative, moderate, or progressive? How important is the preaching? The liturgy?
6. Assess the merits of the three elements von Hügel selected to describe holistic religion. Rank them in order of personal value or preference.
7. Is your relation with God closer to I-Thou or I-It? Explain your answer.
8. How do you "practice the presence of God"?
9. What role does imagination play in your spiritual life? What is your favorite Christian movie, novel, or band? Explain your choices.

4

The Sources of Authority, Part I

Several years ago, nine students, all seniors, joined me around a large old table in a seminar room for a course titled "The Development of Western Christianity." The topic was "The Sources of Authority for Modern Christians." The assigned reading featured the well-known epistemological approach called the Wesleyan Quadrilateral, which enumerates four sources of theology within the Christian tradition—scripture, tradition, reason, and religious experience—and the students were asked to prioritize them and to support their choice.

One fellow, preparing for the Christian ministry, began the discussion by arguing that scripture should be given top priority. The books of the Bible, he stated, are the basis of all Christian belief and practice, since all were inspired directly by God and therefore provide the highest degree of authority. All sources of authority should defer to biblical revelation.

The next student questioned that conclusion. Admitting that scripture is central to Christianity, she noted that the biblical canon was produced by the church and therefore should be included under the category of tradition. In her estimation, tradition, understood as comprising scripture, should have priority for Christian belief and practice.

Another person brought up an equally valid point: tradition, including scripture, comes bound in cultural and historical context and requires interpretation in order to be applied meaningfully to contemporary life. Since interpretation must be filtered through a variety of lenses, including human reason, one could argue that reason stands as the final and foremost source of authority for modern Christians. Several students found this to be persuasive, while recognizing that not all aspects of faith derive from human reason or can be subjected to the authority of reason.

The last person to speak, while agreeing that reason should be held in high esteem, particularly where theological beliefs might be shown to contradict logic or scientific conclusions, noted that logic and reason are not exclusively objective phenomena. Rational people, after all, disagree, and in a global and pluralistic world they increasingly concede that there are—and always have been—many different "rationalities." Thus, while affirming the centrality of reason, she concluded that reason could not claim the final word. In all cases, experience has the first and final word.

We left class pondering that final insight. Does reason, together with scripture and tradition, derive ultimately from experience? Our exercise seemed to support that conclusion, for none of the students had prioritized or substantiated their organization of the four categories in the same way. Subjective experience, it seems, lies at the heart of human consciousness and fashions reality as we know it. What we experience, we are. What we are, we think. What we think, we create. What we create, we become. What we become, we express. And what we express, we experience.

We are left, it seems, with a classical philosophical conundrum. Endings are beginnings, and beginnings are endings. Proofs are based on assumptions, and somehow the entire exercise seems circular.

Faith Seeking Understanding

Complexity, not simplicity, is the hallmark of religious belief among Jews, Christians, and Muslims, and is the result of centuries of the accumulated judgments about the value of certain beliefs and behaviors. However, while religious doctrines do indeed preserve complicated and even competing traditions, they are hardwired to challenge traditional meanings, promote interpretation, and adapt to changing historical circumstances. Monotheistic religions are dynamic traditions, poised between their embrace of the past and the articulation of new meanings. Each of the religious traditions of Judaism, Christianity, and Islam is the product of many distinctive, competing traditions. Because many of these traditions overlap, while retaining unique elements, over time they coalesce to form the larger tradition. This process of consolidation, however, is never complete, for these three religions are constantly interpreting and judging the strands of traditions that shaped them, sometimes in the process creating new traditions. All these strands of

The Sources of Authority, Part I

traditions are kept alive orally or in writing by a community of believers and passed from generation to generation.

Western religions share in some measure a similar predicament. That predicament is best understood as the experience of the capability of religion to supply answers to questions about cosmic order, destiny, truth, and good and evil, while at the same time actively questioning its own legitimacy and adequacy. Religion, in a sense, is a question about the sufficiency of tradition to give meaning to life, as much as it is a lived assent to that tradition.

The study of religion, then, is not focused on a narrow spectrum of culture. Rather, it is an exploration of enduring ways of constructing and representing meaning in human life. Religion, in short, is not a discrete component of human life, separate from other aspects of culture. It is found in the bones and marrow of culture, in the manifold ways that communities and individuals think, act, and feel. Accordingly, learning about religion means discovering the webs of influences, the practical activity, and the aspirations that make us human.

Religion, by its very nature, is forever questing; certainty is therefore not a guarantee. In that regard, many people misunderstand the role of faith, which is more about seeking clarity than certainty, understanding rather than fact. Central to the Christian life is theology, a body of knowledge or ideas about God, the human self, and morality. Where do these ideas originate? On what are they based? And how do they arise? Before engaging with the ideas of Christian theology, scholars make decisions regarding the sources on which these ideas are based, and how they relate to each other. For most Christian theologians, these sources include the Christian Bible, tradition, reason, and experience. Some of the most important debates within Christian theology have concerned the priority that ought to be given to each of these elements. Though not regarded as being of equal importance, each source has a distinct contribution to make within the discipline of theology.

Scripture

A strong connection exists between "scripture" and "tradition," terms of special significance for scholars and others who think historically. People sometimes question which came first, scripture or tradition, but of course, such a question is misleading, for tradition creates scripture. Scripture is itself a process of identity, and hence, a part of tradition. The history of Judaism portrayed in the Hebrew Bible and the history of the early Christian community preserved in the New Testament, a history beginning with creation, Abraham, and Moses and ending with Jesus, Paul, and consummation is a vividly imagined interpretation of the past that has profoundly impacted generations of believers. It should not, however, be seen as a historical record of events from the past. Through its accounts and stories, successive generations of Jews and Christians have found in it the meaning of their own existence in relation to God, others, and the created order.

Because of the literalist reading of scripture by many modern believers, a process both divisive and misleading at best, we begin with a definition of scripture. By scripture we mean a book or a collection of books preserved by religious communities as authoritative sources of teaching or worship. The main point to remember about scriptures is that they are historical objects crafted in human cultures. The texts are preserved by human memory and recorded in human languages, even if they are believed to have come to humans by revelation. Scriptures enjoy special prestige as "holy" or "sacred" texts only because human communities have at some point agreed to treat them in certain ways. Any text regarded as scripture came to be so because a community, formally or informally, so decided. The process that led to authoritative designation is called "canonical," meaning "rule of authority." This decision to accept a text as canonical is often a source of conflict, as different segments of a larger community might dispute whether a particular writing is truly authoritative for all members. Thus it often happens that a text considered as scripture in one community is simply a book in another.

Scripture and tradition, then, are intertwined realities, two sides of a coin. A "canon," or closed collection of scripture, is also a tradition, passed on as a unique and unchangeable record of communal memory, belief, and discipline. Once a traditional literary work becomes scripture, it is usually preserved in a fixed text that cannot be changed or emended. As scriptures are handed on from generation to generation, they must be interpreted so that the unchangeable text continues to remain meaningful to those who revere it. Unfamiliar words cannot be replaced with more up-to-date terms; rather, they must be defined. Obscure concepts or morally troubling events cannot be revised to suit contemporary values; rather, they must be explained. In most cases, translations must be made for those who are unfamiliar with the original language of the scriptural

The Sources of Authority, Part I

texts. All of this work of transmitting the meaning of scriptures is also tradition—the tradition of interpretation.

The decision to regard a text as scripture invariably brings into play the term "tradition." Most simply, tradition means "that which has been handed down from the past." Tradition sustains a book in the life of a religious community long enough for it to acquire the status of scripture. Relatively few examples of writings penned by a known author have attained scriptural authority in that person's own lifetime. Once a traditional literary work becomes scripture, it is usually preserved in a fixed text not to be modified or emended. Scripture and tradition, to summarize, are intertwined realities. Scripture is the collective term for literary traditions that enjoy the veneration of a specific community.

Most religious communities have a list of scriptures considered binding or authoritative. Such a collection is called a "canon," a concept derived from a Greek word meaning "measuring device" or "ruler." As applied to religious literature, it refers to the rule or standard of authority for belief and practice. A "canon," or closed collection of scripture, is thereby a tradition, passed on as a unique and unchangeable record of communal memory, belief, and discipline.

Arriving at a definitive canon or binding list of scriptures involves judging the authenticity, doctrinal soundness, and communal acceptance of texts. While Jews and Christians have a "closed" canon, meaning that no books may be added or deleted from that official collection of writings, this does not mean that their religious communities always agree about which books they include in their respective canons, the form of those books, or the order in which those books occur.

By the start of the first century CE, when Christianity emerged, most Jews subscribed to the special authority of the Torah. Not all accepted the authority of the Prophets (for example the Sadducees did not), but most mainline Jews, including the Pharisees, certainly did. Jesus quoted from some of these books, as did Paul and other New Testament authors, so we can assume that all accepted them as authoritative. The third part, the Writings, was not yet completed in the first century, but one of its major components, the book of Psalms, was already in use in synagogue worship. Indeed, this book was so important that the third part of the Jewish canon could be referred to simply as "the Psalms." This usage is found in Luke's Gospel, from the late first century, which refers to "the Law of Moses, the Prophets, and the Psalms" (Luke 24:44).

The Church Alumni Association

It is no surprise that a faith firmly anchored in the sacred texts of its parent religion would develop scriptures of its own. Christians did develop their own scriptures, but not immediately. The first generation proclaimed its message almost exclusively by word of mouth and saw no pressing need to assemble its own sacred tradition, since it expected Christ to return shortly. As the expected return of Christ was delayed, and as the number of believers continued to expand, the need for written documents became manifest. With the passing of the first generation of Christians, the need arose to preserve those crucial stories and lessons that had given shape to their community; continuity and order were at stake.

Near the end of the first century, Christians were citing Jesus' words and calling them "scripture" (see 1 Tim 5:18). Furthermore, some of Jesus' followers, such as the apostle Paul, understood themselves to be authoritative spokespersons for the truth (Gal 1:8–12). Paul's letters, written occasionally to specific congregations and individuals, were reverently saved and shared with Christians in other places. Shortly thereafter they began to assume the authority of scripture, at least among some Christians (2 Pet 3:16). In fact, Paul's authority was becoming so significant that documents written by others were being ascribed to him (see 2 Thess 2:2; also the pastoral epistles and disputed letters like Hebrews, which some Bibles attribute to Paul). In the next century a host of additional gospels, epistles, and apocalypses appeared, vying for authenticity. The author of Luke's gospel openly admits that "many writers" had preceded him in the attempt to "draw up an account of the things that have happened among us" (Luke 1:1).

By the third century, more than twenty gospels were in circulation, all claiming, like the Gospel of Peter or the Gospel of Philip, apostolic derivation. Notable among them was the Gospel of Thomas, consisting exclusively of isolated saying attributed to Jesus. The abundance of gospels was due mostly to the growth of gnostic sects within Christianity, especially in the second century. The vast majority of gnostics were "dualists," believing that human beings were spiritual entities trapped in an evil material world, and that they could be freed, or saved, only through secret knowledge. They shared in common a tendency to produce texts that claimed to distill new revelation. It is no coincidence that the first lists of scripture began to appear among orthodox scholars and theologians shortly after the emergence of gnostic sects.

The process that led to the formation of the Christian canon is complex but fascinating. The four gospels now found in the New Testament, together with the other canonical writings, may have been produced by diverse, even antithetical communities, but all were viewed to be sufficiently orthodox to make the final cut. However, during the second, third, and fourth centuries, Christians continued to debate the acceptability of certain writings. The arguments centered on three criteria:

- *Apostolicity*: the book in question had to have derived from the initial community of Jesus and his disciples.
- *Orthodoxy*; the book in question had to be valued as inspired and revelatory, that is, as derived directly from God and hence harmonious with the rest of the New Testament.
- *Catholicity*; the book in question had to be accepted and used by a wide range of communities, especially those considered authoritative or apostolic.

At first, a local church would have only a few apostolic letters and perhaps one or two gospels. During the course of the second century most churches came to possess and acknowledge a canon that included the present four gospels, the acts, thirteen letters attributed to Paul, 1 Peter, and 1 John. Seven books still lacked general recognition: Hebrews, James, 2 Peter, 2 and 3 John, Jude, and Revelation. On the other hand, certain Christian writings, such as the first letter of Clement, the letter of Barnabas, the Shepherd of Hermas, and the Didache, were accepted as authoritative by several ecclesiastical writers, though rejected by the majority.

Paradoxically, Marcion, the second-century heretical Christian preacher, was responsible for the first canon of the New Testament. Unable to reconcile the Old Testament's portrayal of God as violent and vengeful with the New Testament's portrayal of God as good and loving, he created a restrictive canon that excluded all of the Old Testament and any Christian literature that had Jewish overtones. Marcion's teaching prompted a hearing before other clergy in Rome that resulted in his condemnation. Soon afterward, other church leaders began to form their own canons or lists of approved books. The most famous of these is the Muratorian Canon, dated to the church at Rome circa 190. It included the four gospels, the Acts of the Apostles, thirteen letters attributed to Paul, Jude, and 1 and 2 John, as well some books that were later excluded, including the Apocalypse of Peter and the Wisdom of Solomon. What is unusual about the latter is that despite being a Jewish work, written prior to the birth of Christianity (in the first century BCE), it was listed as a Christian text.

Strangely, the development of a definitive canon of scripture took orthodox Christians nearly four centuries to complete. The earliest surviving list to include all twenty-seven books now known as the New Testament is from the year 367, appearing in an Easter letter written by Athanasius, bishop of Alexandria, to congregations in the eastern section of the church. In the west, the twenty-seven books of the New Testament were accepted at the subsequent councils of Hippo (393) and Carthage (397).

There is no such thing as a noninterpretive reading of the Bible. Literature invites interpretation; significant literature demands it. This is particularly true of scripture, its truth claims fraught with meaning and therefore open to investigation. It can be said that the history of Christian theology is the history of biblical interpretation.

The earliest Christians had no Bibles to study or read individually. It was the church, and more specifically the religious leaders of that community, that interpreted the scriptures. This was so not only because it had been the church and its leaders that had defined which texts were "scriptural," but also because the texts themselves were not intended as much for private reading as for their suitability for liturgical use. If a document was not considered revelatory, it was not to be read in church. Since most Christians were illiterate and copies of the scriptures were rare, the majority of the faithful could only hear scripture read to them in church, almost always as part of the ritual celebration of the Eucharist. It was principally through the mediation of the clergy and in the restricted context of worship that early Christians could approach scripture.

From the earliest days, Christian leaders formulated theories of biblical interpretation. By the fourth century, clearly defined interpretive theories were already widely accepted by Christian leaders, including that scripture contained four levels of meaning: literal (historical and literal level), allegorical (hidden mystical and spiritual truths), tropological (moral lessons), and anagogical (eschatological level, revealing secrets concerning the afterlife and Christ's future kingdom). While allegorical and other levels of interpretation provided Christian theology with flexibility, giving it the capacity to intertwine written and oral traditions and the ability to adapt to ever-changing situations, in the wrong hands it could be abused, leading to heterodox beliefs and practices. From the fifth through sixteenth centuries, scripture remained firmly in the hands of the church elites who had mastered the accepted exegetical methods. Major controversies were addressed by bishops through synods or councils.

The Sources of Authority, Part I

The Protestant Reformers of the sixteenth century declared that the church had become corrupt because it had buried the truths of scripture beneath layers of humanly devised traditions. Claiming to base their reforms on scripture, the Reformers encouraged the translation of scripture into the vernacular, a process aided by the invention of the printing press. Martin Luther (1485–1546), a first-generation Reformer, believed that faith and the Holy Spirit's illumination were prerequisites for an interpreter of the Bible. He laid down the foundational premise of the Reformation, the principle of *sola scriptura* (scripture alone), the primacy of scripture above all other authorities. Asserting that the Bible should be viewed differently from other literature, he downplayed dependence on church authorities to understand the Bible. Luther also challenged the prevailing "rule of faith," maintaining that rather than the church determining what the scriptures teach, scripture should determine what the church teaches. He also believed that the Bible is a clear book (the "perspicuity" of scripture), in opposition to medieval dogma that the scriptures are so obscure that only the church can uncover their true meaning. He favored a literal understanding of the text, rather than the allegorical method of interpreting scripture, stressing that the interpreter should consider historical conditions, grammar, and context in the process of exegesis.

Probably the greatest exegete of the Reformation was John Calvin (1509–1564), a second-generation reformer. Agreeing in general with the principles articulated by Luther, he too believed that spiritual illumination is necessary and regarded allegorical interpretation as a deceptive device that distorted the clear sense of scripture. Assuming the divine authorship of scripture, he adhered strictly to the principle of harmony, meaning that scripture is its own best interpreter. No passage of scripture should be set up against another; secondary and obscure passages in scripture should always be subject to primary and plain passages. He placed importance on studying the context, grammar, words, and parallel passages, stating that the primary task of an interpreter is to allow the author to speak, rather than to import one's own meaning into the text.

Espousing the priesthood of all believers, the Reformers believed every Christian capable of reading scripture, as guided individually by the Holy Spirit. Rather than leading to unanimity, however, that impetus resulted in further disagreement and fragmentation. Despite their emphasis on scripture as sole authority, the Reformers could not agree with one another on the application of scripture to polity, social issues, and sacramental practices such as baptism or the Eucharist. The unraveling of Christian unity in the sixteenth century led to the emergence of rival communities, each claiming to be the "true" church and to have the correct understanding of scripture.

The Renaissance and the Enlightenment gave rise to ideologies such as humanism, rationalism, skepticism, scientism, and existentialism, each to varying degrees undermining the authority of scripture while simultaneously unleashing a monumental critical effort to ascertain truth in scripture. Searching for truth in scripture, biblical scholars increasingly detected the humanity of the authors who wrote the documents that together constituted the Bible. As Johann Gottfried von Herder argued in the late eighteenth century, the Bible was religious literature, a composite of fact and fiction that was to be analyzed just as one would study any ancient literature. This approach to the Bible came to be known as higher criticism.

With the advent of the modern period, the methodology of biblical interpretation became considerably more complex, reflecting the increased acceptance within academic circles of new methods of interpretation grounded in the assumptions of the Enlightenment. Under the influence of the Enlightenment, four main approaches developed in biblical interpretation.

1. *The rational approach.* Using radical logical criticism, this view regards both Old and New Testaments as resting on a series of supernatural fictions. As such, the supernatural elements of the Bible are not to be taken seriously.

2. *The historical approach.* Treating scripture as an account of Christian origins, this approach attempts to account for the origins of Christianity in purely historical (that is, in secular) terms. Like the rational approach, the historical approach attempts to account for the origins of Judaism and Christianity in purely rational and nonsupernatural terms.

3. *The sociological approach.* By the 1890s, many liberal scholars had lost interest in matters of Christian doctrine or theology, and began to explore the wider category of "religion" or "religious studies" in general. This opened the way for a sociological approach to biblical interpretation, which treated Christianity as a specific example of the category of religion, itself viewed as an aspect of "social history."

4. *The literary approach.* This approach interprets scripture as literature, attempting to do justice to the distinctly literary categories of scripture, particularly its narrative quality.

During the nineteenth and twentieth centuries, various patterns of response countered biblical criticism. One response was the resurgence of *pietism*, a concerted effort to retreat from the chaos and complexity of modernity to a simpler, less rational approach, where scripture was encountered primarily through one's heart. A second response was that of Protestant *fundamentalism*, which countered modernism by reiterating supernaturalism and the inerrancy of scripture. Fundamentalism was joined by Pentecostalism and evangelicalism, movements that likewise embraced conservative biblicism. A third response, *liberalism*, stressed morality in religion and gave precedence to reason over supernaturalism. Liberalism attempted to redefine Christian tradition in such a way as to engage modernity directly. Embracing the discoveries of higher criticism, liberals replaced literalistic approaches to scripture with moral ones. A fourth response, that of *Roman Catholicism*, accepted religious pluralism and modern biblical criticism while encouraging Catholic laity to engage more directly with scripture, arguing that the Catholic Church was the ultimate interpreter of scripture, with the help of the Holy Spirit.

Questions for Discussion and Reflection

1. Name and prioritize the four sources of authority according to their value and usefulness in your decision-making.

2. In today's society, people of faith are often forced to choose between conservative and progressive beliefs and practices. Explain your struggle with these competing forces, and the process that has led you to choose one position over the other.

3. In thinking of religion's role in society, should its primary function be that of an anchor to maintain the status quo, or that of a sail to enable momentum? Explain your answer.

4. What do Christians generally mean when they say that the Bible is "holy"? Explain your answer.

5. In your estimation, what is the role of a scriptural canon? Should the biblical canon remain open, like our Constitution, subject to

The Church Alumni Association

emendation, or should it remain closed? Since no church body ever determined that the canon should be closed, why has tradition supported a "closed" canon?

6. If there is no such thing as a noninterpretive reading of the Bible, what has been your experience with reading and studying the Bible? Do you tend to read for information, for self-understanding, or as a way to relate to God?

7. Of the four major Enlightenment approaches to biblical interpretation mentioned in this chapter, which approach do you find most useful? Why?

5

The Sources of Authority, Part II

HAVING EXAMINED SCRIPTURE AS a source of Christian theology, in this chapter we turn to a consideration of the roles of tradition, reason, and religious experience as sources of religious authority.

Tradition

The word "tradition" comes from the Latin term *traditio*, which means "handing down." The idea is found in the New Testament. Paul, for example, informs his readers that he is handing on to them those core teaching of the Christian faith that he has received from the apostles (1 Cor 15:1–4). The term can refer both to the action of passing teaching on to others—something that Paul insists must be done within the church—and to the body of teachings passed on in this manner. Tradition can be understood as a process as well as a body of teaching.

In response to various controversies within the early church, especially the threat of gnosticism, a "traditional" method of understanding certain passages of scripture began to develop. Scripture could not be allowed to be interpreted in any arbitrary or self-serving way; it had to be interpreted within the context of the historical continuity of the Christian church. This tradition, said to go back to the time of the apostles themselves, became a single-source authority for the developing Christian theology. This emphasis on the authority of scripture was adopted by the mainstream Reformers, who argued that for a doctrine to be orthodox, it had to be shown to be consistent with scripture.

The Church Alumni Association

Earlier, in the fourteenth and fifteenth centuries, a different standard of authority developed, making "tradition" a separate and distinct source of revelation in addition to scripture. Scripture, it was argued, was silent on a number of points, but God had providentially arranged a second source of revelation to supplement this deficiency, a stream of unwritten tradition going back to the apostles themselves. This tradition, passed down from one generation to another within the church, provided a dual-source theory of tradition, based upon two different sources, scripture and unwritten tradition.

Thus, a belief that was not found in scripture could, on the basis of this approach, be justified by an appeal to an unwritten tradition. This position, challenged by the Reformers, was defended strongly at the Council of Trent (1545–1563), which was charged with stating and defending the Catholic position against the threat posed by the Reformation. Trent ruled that scripture could not be regarded as the only source of revelation. The Council therefore argued that scripture and tradition alike were to be viewed as inspired by the same Holy Spirit, and safeguarded and handed down by the same Catholic Church.

When Christianity, particularly Catholic Christianity, claims "tradition" as an authority alongside the Bible, it includes the institutional authority of apostolic succession, the line of bishops traced back to Jesus' disciples, as well as the theological authority of the church fathers and the early church councils, which formulated creedal confessions and statements said to summarize Christian orthodoxy or right belief. The Protestant Reformers, by contrast, significantly downplayed religious tradition in favor of biblical authority. Catholic study of history tends to show a strong correlation between tradition and scripture, whereas Protestant thinkers tend to emphasize discontinuity between the Bible and medieval church tradition, even claiming that Catholicism had corrupted the biblical vision, building extensively on human reason and philosophy and insufficiently on revelation. Of course, given the decades separating the time of Jesus and the writings of the New Testament, scholars question how reliably the New Testament captures the ministry and teachings of Jesus.

While scripture and religious leaders are often venerated as authoritative, in fact, religious authority is actually acknowledged by the religious community itself. Community, then, is the ground of authority. Without community, there would be no scripture, leader, and no house of worship. There are many conceptualizations, many styles of religious authority in

The Sources of Authority, Part II

Judaism, Christianity, and Islam. While there are obvious differences in religious leadership among the three traditions, within each tradition there likewise is a spectrum of ideas about the nature and function of authority. The forms of authority differ because communities differ. Rural settings frequently engender experiences of collective life that differ from those of urban dwellers. Ethnic dissimilarities within a tradition likewise shape social life in different ways. Gender, economic status, and location are among the variables that bear upon group life and can affect the manner in which communities conceive authority.

Members of a religious group experience authority in a way that outsiders might initially find difficult to understand. We should remember that authority is not merely law, doctrine, scripture, religious office, ceremony, or other discrete elements of a tradition. Authority originates in the experience of the individual in community, as part of a rich environment of lived ideas and expectations about both the past and the future.

Is it possible to be a Jew, Christian, or Muslim and yet not stand in any relation to religious authority? The answer to this question is modern and deeply subjective, though throughout the history of these religions, to be Jew, Christian, or Muslim meant to belong to a community.

Reason

The third major source of authority is human reason. As human beings are rational creatures, it is to be expected that reason should play a major role in theology. Christianity, like Judaism and Islam, has been deeply shaped by reason and philosophy. As such, its belief system cannot be reduced to revelation and blind faith. The world of late antiquity that saw the formation of Christianity and rabbinic Judaism was dominated by Greek philosophy, which functioned as the paradigm for rationality. However, the first Christians, while using current Jewish and Greek theological and philosophical categories, perceived a sharp contrast between Greek rationality and divine revelation, leading to considerable debate within Christian circles concerning what their respective roles might be. Early Christian thinkers displayed a variety of attitudes to philosophy and secular culture, including rather uncritical views (Justin Martyr), a rigorous rejection of any role for philosophy in theology (Tertullian), and a willingness to appropriate at least some ideas from secular philosophy (Augustine).

The Church Alumni Association

Beginning in the second century and continuing through the Middle Ages, the Renaissance, and the modern era, leading Christian thinkers sought to weave biblical and philosophical traditions to render them more compatible. Viewing theology as a rational discipline, Thomas Aquinas (1225–1274) used rational arguments to both support and explore the Christian faith. However, Aquinas and the Christian tradition that he represented did not limit Christianity to what could be ascertained by reason. Faith goes beyond reason, having access to truths and insights of revelation that reason alone could not comprehend. For scholastic thinkers, theology was a *scientia*, that is, a rational discipline, using reason to extend what is known by revelation.

After 1300, Christian theologians became increasingly dependent on Greek philosophy to provide a basis for Christian theology. Opposing this approach, the Reformers resolved to reverse the trend, advocating a return to a biblical worldview in which scripture alone was authoritative, not scripture and tradition, as emphasized by scholastic Catholic thinkers.

During these periods, extensive debate occurred in the Western world regarding faith, revelation, and reason. During the Enlightenment, some well-known conflicts developed, particularly as reason came to be defined in terms of scientific reason. Initially, by the middle of the seventeenth century, an attitude developed in certain European circles that declared the rationality of Christian belief. Seeking to secure faith squarely upon rational foundations, thinkers such as Lord Herbert of Cherbury (1583–1684) sought to show that every aspect of Christian belief derived from human reason.[1]

This approach had two major consequences. It effectively reduced Christianity to those ideas that could be proved by reason, and it elevated reason over revelation. Eventually, this rationalistic position was pushed to its logical outcome. Finding many ideas in Christianity to be inconsistent with reason, it found such beliefs irrational. This approach, often termed "Enlightenment rationalism," led to previously unknown views of God, such as deism, a stepping-stone for some to skepticism and for others to atheism. In the process, God came increasingly to be described in human

---

1. Beginning in the seventeenth century, Enlightenment thinkers started to draw a contrast between "revealed" religion and "natural" religion. Viewing revealed religion as unique to Christianity and natural religion as the original religion of humankind, Lord Herbert described natural religion as universal, rational, and compatible with natural laws. However, influenced by Christianity, he attributed belief in a single supreme being as inherent to natural religion, including belief in immortal human souls that would be punished or rewarded according to their actions in this life.

The Sources of Authority, Part II

categories, rationally and morally, projected to infinity. Some, like the early American president Thomas Jefferson, used eighteenth-century French rationalism to dismiss doctrines such as the Trinity or the deity of Christ, viewing Jesus as a simple but rational Jewish teacher, who taught a reasonable gospel about a rational idea of God.

A direct consequence of this approach was the movement in New Testament studies known as the "quest of the historical Jesus." This quest, which dates from the late eighteenth century, was based upon the belief that the New Testament got Jesus entirely wrong. The real Jesus was a simple Galilean teacher who taught entirely sensible ideas based on reason. In his celebrated work, *Religion within the Limits of Reason Alone*, the German philosopher Immanuel Kant (1724–1804) argued powerfully for the priority of reason and conscience over the authority of Jesus.

In the twentieth and twenty-first centuries, new ideas emerged about geometry, biology, and physics, questioning whether a universal and necessarily true system of reality could be based on reason alone. This same argument was also applied to philosophy and theology. Where once it was argued that there was only one single rational model or methodology, postmodern thinkers such as Alasdair MacIntyre (born 1929) and Hans-Georg Gadamer (1900–2002) increasingly argued that there are—and always have been—many different "rationalities," each of which has to be respected in its own right. Thus there is today no privileged vantage point, no universal concept of "reason," which can pass judgment on rationality.

Such thinking invariably leads to the question, "Is there such a thing as religious reason?" Philosophers of religion explore the relation of reason and religion in a variety of ways. Current thinkers such as Alvin Plantinga and Nicholas Wolterstorff view religious doctrines as beliefs that can be experientially and communally justified and, therefore, considered rational. Others argue that religious language is primarily metaphorical, and should not be understood factually or literally. Postliberal theologian George Lindbeck, for example, notes various ways to think about religious doctrines, distinguishing between cognitive approaches, experiential-expressive approaches, and cultural-linguistic approaches. In other words, doctrines can be viewed in at least four different ways: (1) definitively, that is, conclusively and absolutely, (2) determinatively, as patterns that shape the lives and thought of believers, (3) culturally, as pictures or frames through which we see the world, or (4) literarily, as analogous to poetry in their capacity for opening up new ways to see the world.

However viewed, one thing we notice repeatedly is that religious thought is and should be much more than mindless creedal affirmation, for it contains within it a self-correcting and self-critical element. While religious belief, however rationally justified, will likely never be universally accepted, for many religious philosophers and theologians, faith must be self-critical, and such critical thinking is the one mark of rationality that brings religion as close to universal as it can get.

Religious Experience

"Experience" is an imprecise term. In its broad sense, the word is related to "tradition," only applied individually. In this regard, experience means "an accumulated body of knowledge arising through first-hand encounter with life." Over time, the term came to refer to the inner life of individuals, akin to spirituality. In the eighteenth century, emphasis on the importance of inward, subjective religious experience came to characterize Methodism. As we noted earlier, the term "the Wesleyan Quadrilateral" came to be used when referring to the grouping of scripture, tradition, reason, and experience.

The first three elements reflect John Wesley's (1703–1791) insistence that the task of interpreting the Bible was to be aided by the collective Christian wisdom of past ages as well as being protected from extreme or obscure approaches by means of critical reason. Most importantly, for Wesley, the message of scripture must be received in the heart by a living faith, which experiences God as present.

In his discussion of experience as a source of theology, Alister McGrath describes two main approaches to the question of the experience as a source of authority, which we might call naturalistic or humanistic and supernaturalistic or spiritualistic.[2] The humanistic approach has attractive elements, for it views all religious knowledge through the lens of human experience, something common to all humanity rather than the preserve of an exclusive group. This view suggests that all the world religions are basically human responses to the same religious experience. Building on this view, Christians ought to seek not what is distinctive about Christianity but rather to reflect upon this common human experience, in the knowledge that the same experience underlies other world religions.

While attractive for theological pluralism, McGrath points out that this view lacks empirical verification. "Religious experience," it seems, is

2. McGrath, *Christian Theology*, 148.

The Sources of Authority, Part II

a hopelessly vague idea. As George Lindbeck points out in *The Nature of Doctrine*, appealing to the "experiential-expressive theory of doctrine," the notion that all religions have a "common core experience" of truth, reality, or of the Ultimate is an ultimately unverifiable hypothesis.

The supernaturalistic approach regards experience as something that needs to be interpreted. Christian theology (seen as based on divine revelation rather than on human intuition, reason, or experience), is here understood to provide a framework by which the ambiguities of experience may be interpreted. Unfortunately, for many Christians, this view is built on the fall-redemption model, also known as original sin or "the heaven-and-hell framework," a model that has dominated Christian anthropology, theology, biblical studies, theological education, and even sociology for centuries.

What would happen to your faith—and your perspectives, priorities, lifestyle, even your attitudes—if you took as theological starting point the reality of original goodness ("original blessing") rather than original sin? The fall-redemption tradition, based on patriarchal models that are dualistic and outdated, comprises four central elements: the afterlife, sin and forgiveness, Jesus' death for the sin of humanity, and belief.

According to this model, heaven is the goal of life, the primary reason for being Christian. Sin is the central issue in one's life, and forgiveness is the solution. Because humans are sinners, they deserve to be punished. However, Jesus died for our sins, thereby making forgiveness possible. Those who affirm ("believe in") this framework and accept ("have faith in") Christ's gift of forgiveness are assured eternal life with God in heaven. The fall-redemption framework views the Christian life as centered in belief now for the sake of eternal salvation. What is most important about Jesus is not his life but his death, and belief in him is central to one's eternal salvation. The goal of life is a blessed afterlife, which can only be gained through Christ's work of salvation, received by faith, and maintained through worship and the sacramental life.

Critics view the fall-redemption model as guilt-ridden and therefore as psychologically flawed, in that it tends to devalue life and deprive it of much of its vitality, joy, and goodness. This framework is also said to be based on a false and unbiblical meaning of key concepts such as salvation, sacrifice, mercy, repentance, redemption, and faith, which in the Bible are concerned with temporal safety, peace, and wellbeing and rarely refer to heaven or the afterlife. In addition, this perspective is viewed by many historians and theologians as having adversely contributed to racism, sexism, nationalism, exclusivism, and other harmful ideologies.[3]

By contrast, the creation-centered tradition, which is more ancient, emphasizes goodness, blessing, joy, creativity, play, innocence, and pleasure rather than sin and guilt, and is committed to social transformation and justice-making. Because the fall/redemption tradition considers all nature "fallen" and does not seek God in nature but inside the individual soul, it tends to ignore science or be hostile to it.

According to theologian Matthew Fox, author of *Original Blessing* and other creation-centered books: "To recover a spiritual tradition in which the goodness of creation and the study of creation matters would be to inaugurate new possibilities between spirituality and science that would shape the paradigms for culture, its institutions, and its people. These paradigms would be powerful in their capacity to transform. For if wisdom comes from nature and religious traditions . . . then what might happen if science and religious traditions agreed to birth together instead of ignoring, fighting, or rejecting one another? Is not recovering a creation-centered spirituality recovering two sources of wisdom at once, that of nature via science and that of nature via religious traditions? The creation-centered tradition seems to combine the best of both worlds in our search for wisdom today."[4]

Reconfiguring Christianity's predominant dogmatic paradigm—replacing the fall/redemption model with the creation-centered model—can make a great difference in one's faith and lifestyle. Our focus as Christians should be on the here-and-now, on our "this-worldly" task and journey. In my estimation, focusing on sin as a path to damnation and on salvation as a path to the afterlife is peripheral to Christianity and serves as a distraction from the urgent tasks at hand. Furthermore, to quote award-winning author Robert Wright, "religions that have failed to align individual salvation with social salvation have not, in the end, fared well. And, like it or not, the social system to be saved is now a global one. Any religion whose prerequisites for individual salvation don't conduce to the salvation of the whole world is a religion whose time has passed."[5]

---

3. For additional information on the "heaven-and-hell framework" and on how particular Christian words have lost their original meaning and power, see Borg, *Speaking Christian*, 10–17.

4. Fox, *Original Blessing*, 11–12.

5. Wright, *Evolution of God*, 430.

The Sources of Authority, Part II

Questions for Discussion and Reflection

1. While for some Christians the Bible can be said to have replaced "tradition" as the primary authority, the Bible appears to be a subset of tradition, at least theoretically, and hence never completely autonomous. In your estimation, can the Bible ever exist as an authority separate from or over tradition? Explain your answer.

2. Explain and assess the merits of the statement, for people of faith, "Community . . . is the [ultimate] ground of authority." If this is true, is religious authority ultimately arbitrary and subjective? If so, is there any objective basis for truth and authority in human society?

3. Explain the history of Christianity's subtle "dance" with reason. If religion can be portrayed as rational, is there ultimately any substantial difference between philosophical and theological perspectives on religion?

4. If reason is an essential aspect of modernity, explain the merits of the conundrum posed by postmodern thinkers who argue that there are—and always have been—many different and competing "rationalities." If this be true, how do you answer the question, "Is there such a thing as religious reason"?

5. In religious epistemology, how does "experience" function as a source of authority? In the current debate, do you side with those who argue that "religious experience" is a hopelessly vague idea, or with those who argue that all religions have a "common core experience" that qualifies as an objective source of authority? Explain your answer.

6. If we can talk of a Christian or a biblical core of belief, should it be based on fall-redemption (original sin) models or on creation-centered (original blessing) models? Explain your answer.

6

The Crisis of Authority in Modernity

SPIRITUALITY IS UNIVERSAL AND timeless. The first humans—our earliest ancestors—were deeply spiritual, and human beings have been spiritual ever since. While we sometimes tend to think of the first humans as primitive—they were certainly primitive technologically—it is better to call them primal, for they came first, and their worldview was more sophisticated than that of many moderns. Everything for them was religious, for they thought of nature as imbued with sanctity. Furthermore, they viewed life and nature with wonder and reverence, for they envisioned no line separating the visible world from the more real spiritual world that surrounds and nurtures the physical realm. Primal peoples were concerned (and continue doing so, for their holistic views are perpetuated in primal societies still found across the globe, such as in Native American groups and societies found throughout North and South America) with the maintenance of personal, social, and cosmic harmony, because for them all things are related.

Primal people are embedded in their world. Their rituals are not attempts to stand apart from or to control nature, for primal people view humanity and nature as belonging to a single order. Rather than attempting to produce extraordinary effects or control nature magically, primal rites focus on maintaining the patterns of nature; they are rituals of cooperation rather than of coercion or manipulation. While articulating basic human needs, these rituals also sustain confidence in the processes of nature, spiritually conceived, and renew hope for the future.

What holds true for individuals applies to institutions as well. Individuals change and adapt, and so must institutions, if they are to remain relevant. As societies grow, develop, and change, so religions evolve, adapt, and change. Western Christianity emerged primarily from Judaism and indirectly from pagan religions current in the eastern Mediterranean world, themselves an outgrowth of primal spirituality.

Once Christianity established a foothold in the Greco-Roman world, it can be said to have progressed through four stages:

1. *Revealed religion.* This formal, institutional, and hierarchical phase, often called Christendom, was modeled on the Roman imperial system. Premodern in nature, this Western religious ethos focused primarily on scripture, rituals, dogmas, and clerical intermediaries, and on the spiritual experiences they engender. Despite undergoing denominational fracture, this model continued during the medieval and Reformation eras.

2. *Enlightened religious movements.* Modern in nature, this Western religious ethos focused on individuals who valued rationality and the scientific method. Emphasizing natural reason and universal truth over revealed truth, this stage flourished during the Enlightenment. During this period, scholars studied religion and the Bible as products of human history rather than as divinely revealed entities.

3. *Fundamentalist religious movements.* Viewed as a return to revealed religion, this Western religious ethos is primarily a reactionary approach to modernity. A product of modernity, this mindset places high value on its own perceived rationality. Fundamentalism flourished in the nineteenth and twentieth centuries and continues to be attractive to traditional Christians today.

4. *Postmodern spirituality.* Focusing primarily on holistic spiritual experiences, this perspective emphasizes global and pluralistic values, viewing truth as inherently ambiguous and knowledge as relative, subjective, and fallible rather than certain and absolute. This Western religious ethos began in the twentieth century and is a predominant form of spirituality in the twenty-first century.

Medieval Epistemology

Augustine's epic work on the church, *The City of God*, arguably Christianity's earliest greatest philosophical treatise, was published in 426 CE and took Augustine at least a decade to write. Written in response to the Visigoth sacking of Rome in 410, *The City of God* was Augustine's attempt to rebut the widespread claim that Rome's demise was punishment for abandoning the traditional gods in favor of the new state religion, Christianity. Augustine answered, to the contrary, that Rome became Christian too late. The sins of centuries were so engraved in Roman society that they eroded her strength, and therefore she fell under barbarian attack.

According to Augustine, human society is composed of two cities, distinguished by two loves: the heavenly city (the "City of God," characterized by the love of God) and the earthly city (the "City of Man," characterized by the love of Self). He envisioned these "cities" or "loves," operative throughout human history, as abstract in nature, and cautioned that they should not be identified strictly with the visible church or state. Augustine viewed these cities as universal in scope, meaning that all human beings fall within one of these jurisdictions. Thinking imaginatively, Augustine noted that these societies had their origin after the expulsion of Adam and Eve from the Garden of Eden, in the ensuing offerings (lifestyles) of Cain and Abel, descendants of the earliest humans (the story is recorded in Genesis 4). God refuses Cain's offering, presumably because it results from impure motives, but accepts Abel's sacrifice. The result—the first fratricide—proves disastrous for family and social life. Both "cities," anticipating human history, progress along separate paths toward radically different ends. Unlike Abel, the members of God's city nevertheless remain in the world, their function a leavening or renewing force.

While modern people might dismiss Augustine's portrayal of history as simplistic, his perspective nevertheless raises questions about the church's nature, its role in society, and whether the church has lived up to its nature and destiny as God's new creation. These are our concerns as well.

As we noted earlier, in his *Confessions*, Augustine declared the human goal as knowing and loving the God who created us. In religious traditions, knowing God is considered the highest and most important form of knowing. Hence, it should come as no surprise that in the monotheistic traditions, epistemology (theories of knowing) reigns supreme.

To know God, however, is not a simple or singular endeavor, for such knowing involves not only theories of God's nature, but also theories of the structure and nature of the human self and of the world. In this regard, various questions arise immediately. For example, is the world purposeful or meaningful? If it is part of a created cosmos, is it the stage for the outworking of the divine drama of sin and salvation? Furthermore, is the cosmos so constructed—are the natural and the divine so intimately interwoven—as to reflect the purpose and will of God? In addition, are humans only physical or also spiritual by nature, possessing body and soul? If so, how we think about the world and the self clearly influences how we think about God.

In the Christian philosophical tradition, scholars often have equated mind and soul, meaning humans can know God intellectually, that is, with the "mind's eye" (with the soul or intellect), rather than empirically, that is, with the "body's eye" (with the senses). Seeing with the "mind's eye" (also called "intellectual vision") occurs often in ordinary situations, when, for instance, after not understanding something, you finally exclaim, "Oh, that is what it means. Now I get it!" This type of knowing, combining yet transcending intellect and intuition, may be called "mystical" or "spiritual." Together with sensible (physical) and rational forms of intelligence, it too is a means of knowing and loving God.

Despite the existence of diverse theologies and beliefs in the Christian Middle Ages, two theologians dominated medieval epistemology: Augustine (354-430), bishop of Hippo, and Thomas Aquinas (1225-1274), the great Dominican scholar. While both appealed to biblical revelation, they used the ideas of Greek philosophers to interpret this revelation.

Augustine's epistemology had faith as its foundation, faith based on divine revelation. Since human beings use reason to understand truth they receive by faith, belief is the prerequisite for further understanding. Reason is not sufficient, for because of human sinfulness, information received by the senses is prone to error. However, blind faith or belief is not sufficient. For Augustine, the goal of faith is not belief but rather understanding. In his commentary on the gospel of John he wrote, "Understanding is the reward of faith. Therefore seek not to understand in order that you may believe, but believe in order that you may understand." Augustine eventually shortened this into the motto, *credo ut intelligam*: "I believe in order that I might understand."

For Augustine, if God and the Bible are accepted as epistemological starting points, then believers must seek to understand all truth in light of God. Human beings, thus, are not self-sufficient and autonomous, but rather are dependent upon God's grace, which sheds light or "illumines" their understanding. Whereas autonomous human thinking is limited by human sinfulness, the grace of God can transform the mind into an instrument that moves from faith to understanding.

Like Augustine, Thomas Aquinas intended to show that philosophy need not lead to a rejection of the Christian faith. However, unlike Augustine, Thomas's system based the Christian faith on rational foundations. For Aquinas, faith and revelation are correlated, not antithetical. While revelation might reveal truths that transcend reason, it would not contradict reason. Aquinas, for example, would have considered it inconceivable that reason could lead to atheism. As he demonstrated in his "Five Proofs," he believed that the world is so structured and the human mind so constituted that systematic reflection will lead all who reflect rationally on the data of sense experience to believe in God's existence. Given their different starting points and their disagreements on methodology, Augustine and Aquinas's epistemological approaches are antithetical. Whereas Augustine had said, "I believe in order that I may understand," Thomas's motto was *intelligo ut credam*, "I understand in order that I might believe." Since systematic reflection on the data of experience are not self-explanatory, humans must assume or postulate that there is a transcendent being on which these data depend for their very existence.

Whereas philosophers call Augustine's approach "revealed or supernatural theology," they call Aquinas's approach "natural theology." Nevertheless, for Aquinas, the distinction between the natural and the supernatural is not nearly as strong as it is for most of us today. Aquinas maintained a cosmos in which nature could not be understood fully apart from God's grace. In the periods between the thirteenth and seventeenth centuries—the period of the Renaissance and the Reformation—a new cosmology emerged in the West, one that separated God more radically from nature.

Religion and Modernity

What is it human beings do when they profess belief in God? When they pray? When they join with others in rituals of worship? Western philosophers and religious thinkers have asked these questions for centuries. However, in the seventeenth century, with the advent of modernity, the nature of these inquiries changes.

When we use the term "modernity," we are speaking of a historical period characterized by advances in science, philosophy, and politics.

The Crisis of Authority in Modernity

Modernity also marks a new attitude toward the world and humanity's place in it, where intellectual and cultural authority is no longer located in past traditions or in divine revelation but in our exercise of reason, and where humanity's sense of indebtedness to the past is replaced by confidence in its ability to shape the world for future generations.

In this context, Western intellectuals began to ask new questions about God, faith, and religion. How do we know that God exists? Can reason defend any of the assertions about God and the world claimed by religious traditions? Is religion a force for good in human life, or is it something that belongs to a past age, a symptom of the infancy of humanity? Prior to the modern period, few serious thinkers questioned the existence of God or the importance of religion for human life. For medieval thinkers, the truth had been revealed, and the task of philosophy and religion was to understand this truth. They were engaged in the project of "theology" as "faith seeking understanding." However, once the Protestant Reformation of the sixteenth century divided Western Christianity, and with the successes of scientific inquiry into the workings of nature, such thinkers as René Descartes (1596–1650) sought to ground knowledge in "natural reason." Increasingly, they came to believe that they could identify a universal human rationality that worked independently of faith. With this development, modern philosophy separated itself from theology and gave birth to a new way of thinking about religion. Even though many philosophers continued to defend religion as "reasonable," others criticized it as irrational and harmful and developed methods for explaining religion as a psychological or social, rather than a divine, phenomenon. Atheism became a real possibility and criticism of religion became an intellectual responsibility.

Modernity and the Realm of Reason

With the birth of modern science in the seventeenth century, as human knowledge and technological accomplishment led to improvements in the human condition, the realm of faith gradually succumbed to the realm of reason. During the eighteen and nineteenth centuries, a growing minority of scholars and thinkers came to denounce religion, viewing it as irrational, illusory, and even as dangerous. While some philosophers continued to argue for the value and necessity of religion, others just as carefully argued against it, predicting its diminishment and eventual demise.

The Church Alumni Association

Modernity—a creation of the West, essentially over the past four hundred years—is a cultural mindset that increasingly persuaded leading thinkers to turn from the authority of past tradition to the authority of reason. We see this most clearly in the period we call the Enlightenment, a period in European history from roughly the late seventeenth century to the end of the eighteenth century. The modern ethos can be summarized in the injunction of the philosopher Immanuel Kant: "dare to know." In other words, don't take things by faith, from religious authority, but ask questions, become educated, and above all, use reason. Whereas traditional authorities looked to the past for guidance and truth, modern thinkers looked to the future, thereby remaining open to the realization of their full potential. For them, modernity meant progress.

In the past, thinkers used the term "modern," not to describe that which was simply current or up to date, but rather a cultural era. As way of thinking, modernity embraced a plethora of cultural, intellectual, political, scientific, and technological changes that radically transformed Western civilization. In the wake of this new and revolutionary mindset, people began to think of themselves as standing at the beginning of a new era of history. They saw themselves breaking with the past and forging a new vision of what it means to be human. However, as with any new era of major social and cultural change, this vision occurred in the context of debate.

Which aspects of the past remain important? What does the future hold? What does it mean to be human, or in this case, to be modern? At the center of these debates was the question of religion. Is religion a part of the past to be rejected, or can one be modern and religious simultaneously? While asking such questions, we need to be aware that not only were decisions about religion central to the debates of the eighteenth and nineteenth centuries, but that the very concept of religion itself, as we use it today, was a product of this debate. That is to say, "religion" as an idea emerged as people struggled with the question of what it means to be modern.

If you had asked people in premodern Europe if they were religious, they would have thought you were asking whether they were monks or nuns. To be religious in this sense meant you were part of a Catholic order. Today, of course, we use this term differently, thinking of a set of religious beliefs and practices but also of institutions that constitute a sphere of life that we distinguish from other spheres of life, such as politics, art, or science. It is to those thinkers of the eighteenth and nineteenth centuries that we owe this way of thinking we call "modern," who started looking at the world in a new way, dividing things differently, categorizing the world in a new way, and part of this process was to make the conceptual distinction between what we call religion and other aspects of life.

While the question of whether it is possible to be modern and religious at the same time was central to Enlightenment thinkers, the question remains with us today. However, if you had asked intellectuals in the mid-twentieth century—say in the late 1960s and early 1970s—that question, they would have said that modernity meant the gradual decline and possibly even the elimination of religion. Viewed in the context of that period, what scholars would have offered was a version of the secularization thesis, meaning that in the modern world religion plays a decreasing and lesser role in the public—and especially in the political—sphere, temporarily confined to the private sphere of the family and the individual before likely withering away altogether.

However, if you put this question to intellectuals today, fifty years later, many will give a different answer. As we know, religion has been central in the news over that period, a major factor in Muslim countries such as Iraq, Iran, and Saudi Arabia and to a lesser extent in places like India and Central and South America. We know that religion is central in the cultural wars in the United States as well, particularly regarding such issues as abortion, stem cell research, evolution, or the separation of church and state. Since the 1940s, evangelicalism has played a major role in American politics, including in the election of presidents such as Jimmy Carter, Ronald Reagan, and Donald Trump. In this regard, we may consider also the social influence in America by Jerry Falwell's Moral Majority and Pat Robertson's Christian Broadcasting Network. While religion plays a central role for evangelical Christians, it does so for millions of nonevangelical Christians as well, many affirming its public and even political function in American life.

Must religion build barriers between people, we wonder, or can it build bridges as well? Like life itself, religion is a messy and complicated phenomenon, at times bound up with the worst in human thought and behavior and at other times bound up with the best.

During the sixteenth and into the seventeenth centuries, Europe was beset by a series of wars that pitted Catholics against Protestants and new economic and social structures against established structures. This also was the period of the Scientific Revolution, associated with such figures as Copernicus, Galileo, and Newton, through whom a radically new picture of the cosmos and the "natural laws" within it took hold of European intellectual culture. These achievements led French rationalist René Descartes and other philosophers to rethink the nature of intellectual activity and, thus, to seek new foundations for human knowledge in reason rather than in tradition and revelation.

By 1650, following the Reformation and the breakup of Christendom, many Europeans were demanding new ways to think about the church, including new ways to relate religion, politics, and society. New conceptions of the cosmos challenged the classic medieval view of the church and provided new ways to think about God, the self, and religion, based upon the authority of science, philosophy, and reason rather than divine revelation as mediated by church theologians or the clergy. This situation produced a crisis of authority in Europe. One solution, provided by Enlightenment thinkers such as Descartes, Locke, and Voltaire, was to elevate human reason over divine revelation, the individual thinker over the church's doctrines, councils, creeds, and papal decrees.

Enlightenment thought reached a culmination in the work of the German philosopher Immanuel Kant (1724–1804). Denying revelation as a means of attaining certainty, Kant deified reason, an innate way of knowing, as the only epistemological authority. For Kant, scripture should be read and interpreted morally, for, as he argued, "the moral improvement of humanity contributes the real end of religions of reason." Disagreeing with the Reformers and their biblical predecessors, he argued that moral reason, not the Holy Spirit, should be the interpreter of scripture. God, for Kant, is unknowable, and therefore relegated to the position of a postulate, that is, a useful idea for morality.

Kant spoke of two kinds of knowledge, (a) knowledge of what is, by which he meant scientific knowledge, given to the understanding through sense impressions, and (b) knowledge of what ought to be, by which he meant innate moral knowledge. Kant wanted norms, but he looked within rather than externally to find them. Kant focused on morality, finding within human beings a universal moral law that he called the "categorical imperative." Arguing that natural reason demands virtue, he found that finite beings, due to their limitations, regularly fall short of the demands of the moral law because their natural desire for happiness affects their moral will. Because virtue and happiness do not necessarily coincide, humans need help and resolve. For moral progress to be possible, Kant argued that believers should organize and attend church.

Kant is often seen as a bridge to religious subjectivism and existentialism. He did not believe humans could know spiritual reality directly; rather, they could only postulate it by faith, that is, indirectly and subjectively. In Kant, Aquinas's certainty was greatly eroded. Lacking natural revelation, the gulf between the natural and supernatural had become a chasm.

Two cultural and religious movements—pietism and romanticism—shaped Western religious thought after Kant. Both movements criticized the abstract rational universalism of the Enlightenment, doing so by emphasizing personal experience. Romantics and pietists argued that God could be experienced directly. Romanticism, a philosophical, literary, and artistic movement, sought to overturn what it perceived as the sterility and abstractions of the Enlightenment focus on rationality. It stressed the individual as a feeling, creative subject, and the lived experience of religious faith. Theologically, pietist thinkers emphasized the spiritual and moral regeneration that results from one's direct experience of Jesus Christ.

Whereas Enlightenment thinkers focused on reason as the answer to the religious conflicts of post-Reformation Europe, the pietists saw one of the main sources of conflict in ecclesiology and denominationalism, rooted in rigid adherence to doctrinal and theological belief. Consequently, the pietists turned to religious experience and the "religion of the heart." While the main task for early Enlightenment thinkers was to demonstrate the compatibility of reason and religion, for pietists, the primary task was to provide assurance of salvation. Pietism played a major role in German Lutheranism, in the Methodism of John Wesley, and in American evangelicalism.

Pietism was clearly a religious movement designed to rejuvenate and invigorate the lives of everyday Christians. Romanticism, however, was an artistic, literary, and philosophical movement, largely secular in nature and only tenuously connected to established religious traditions. Its exponents emphasized the spontaneous, emotional, and creative side of human life. Some romantics dismissed religion altogether, whereas others saw "real" religion in an artistic-contemplative connection with the world and in the idea that the divine works through creative imagination.

Enlightenment thinkers, like many traditional Christians, stressed the rational self and therefore abstract, formal, universal aspects of the self. In contrast, romantic and pietist thinkers placed greater value on individual belief and experience. In the romantics Rousseau and Coleridge, we find appeals to "conscience" and "imagination" respectively, which serve as points of contact, even of mystical union, with the divine. Romantic thinkers placed a strong value on the individual's particular place in the cosmos, a unique expression of the energy or life of the world soul or nature. For them, church gatherings, if they existed at all, should ideally be conducted outdoors, in nature's own cathedral.

The romantic and pietist visions of religious experience are uniquely combined in the thought of Friedrich Schleiermacher (1768–1834), often called "the father of modern theology." Defending religion against its modern critics, Schleiermacher argued that religion was not primarily a matter of intellect or even of morality, but rather was grounded in intuition or feeling about the whole of reality. For Schleiermacher, religion is the experience or perception that connects human beings to the universe and makes us receptive to its beauty and vitality. For Christians, this perception becomes concrete as a sense of "absolute dependence" on God. In his groundbreaking 1799 book, *On Religion: Speeches to Its Cultured Despisers*, Schleiermacher argued, in terms understandable to leading figures in the romantic circles of Germany, why religion is not something to be ignored or despised, but rather is at the heart of a vibrant, thoughtful, and creative life.

To make his point, Schleiermacher agreed with his audience that the orthodoxies and traditions of existing religions, as well as the overly rationalistic Enlightenment philosophies, were only faint shadows of authentic experiential religions. He urged the despisers of organized religion to look to their own experience to find the essence of religion, which he called "the sense and taste for the infinite." For Schleiermacher, the essence of religion is neither knowing nor being, but rather sensing and feeling. He wanted to show the detractors of organized religion that the experience of the infinite is part of every human experience. For Schleiermacher, to live fully, with feeling, curiosity, and imagination, embracing all individuals, objects, and experiences as aspects of the divine whole, is the essence of religion, of what we today call spirituality.

With Schleiermacher, G. W. F. Hegel (1770–1831) is considered one of the most formative religious thinkers of the nineteenth century. Seeking to overcome the static rationalism of the Enlightenment, Hegel argued that history is the process whereby Absolute Spirit (or God) empties itself in creation. In his book, *The Phenomenology of Spirit* (1806), Hegel developed what he called the "dialectic," a three-part process whereby *Geist* (the Absolute Spirit or World Soul) achieves self-consciousness in and through the historical development by which human beings achieve self-consciousness about themselves and reality. The notion that the life of the World Spirit develops together with human knowledge is perhaps Hegel's most revolutionary concept.

Affirming Christianity as the "consummate religion," Hegel viewed the history of religion as the story not only of humanity, but also of this Spirit. Unlike Kant's philosophy, which viewed knowledge and reality in static terms, Hegel understood reality and human knowledge of reality as something that evolves or develops over time. The Christian doctrine of the Trinity illustrates Hegel's tripartite structure of reality. Spirit, or God, begins as an undifferentiated, eternal essence, and then differentiates, separating from itself to produce the cosmos, world, and humanity. The development within Spirit follows the dialectic, in which thesis (Absolute Spirit) is negated by antithesis (creation), and then taken up into a higher synthesis (divine self-consciousness).

The Christian doctrine of incarnation is a way of representing God's emptying into the world, and resurrection, representing the embodiment of God as Holy Spirit in the Christian community, illustrates the synthesis, whereby Spirit is reconciled to itself through the world and, particularly, through the development of human self-consciousness. In other words, the process by which human self-knowledge and knowledge of the world develops is the same process by which Spirit comes to self-consciousness. Thus, Spirit is reconciled in humanity. For Hegel, the goal of the human story is the goal of Spirit; the end of the story of Spirit is the divinization of human community.

The spiritual freedom of Protestantism that erases the boundaries between church and world and makes priests of all believers embodies the realization that the divine is not limited to the church, but rather thrives in progressive human community. In short, theology is mirrored in anthropology; in the end, human self-consciousness is God's self-consciousness.

The contributions of Kant, Schleiermacher, and Hegel laid the groundwork for a theological approach known as "liberal theology." Each of these thinkers contributed a new understanding of faith. Kant made room for rational faith in God, Schleiermacher made feeling and religious piety a point of immediate connection with the infinite, and Hegel argued for the rational apprehension of God in the whole of reality.

The Church Alumni Association

The Loss of Biblical Authority

During the Enlightenment, thinkers began studying the Bible as a historical document. Applying the verification criterion of science and reason, some thinkers questioned the accuracy of historical events in the Bible, such as miracles. In the nineteenth century, primarily under the influence of Hegel, historical awareness raised a new set of challenger for religious thinkers. Foremost among those was the emergence of the historical-critical method of studying the Bible, known as higher criticism. This led to studying the Bible as a human, historically constructed text. This approach to scripture raised questions about the authorship, interpretation, and authority of scripture, and the importance of distinguishing the "historical Jesus" behind the gospels from the "Jesus of faith."

In 1883, for example, Julius Wellhausen put forward the "documentary hypothesis," which argued that the books of the Pentateuch, including Genesis, were constituted by four different sources, all later than Moses, blended together in the fifth and fourth centuries BCE. Earlier, David Strauss published *The Life of Jesus* (1835), in which he argued that careful study of the New Testament reveals little if any evidence that Jesus was divine. Strauss argued that the biblical authors thought in mythical (poetic or figurative) rather than historical terms, and when scholars separate myth from history in the Bible, little remains to support Christian doctrines of Jesus or even Christian doctrines as a whole.

Following Hegel, Strauss argued that mythical language is central to all religious language, and that what Christianity communicates is a kind of truth, only not a historical, scientific, or factual truth. This approach to the Bible proved extremely controversial, not only because it challenged basic claims made by Christians and Jews, but because it led to treating the Bible as a human book and, thus, to treat religion and history as a human, rather than a divine, phenomenon.

Questions for Discussion and Reflection

1. Epistemologically speaking, what does it mean to "know God"? Is such "knowledge" possible for human beings? Explain your answer.
2. In your own words, describe the fourfold progression of Christianity in medieval and modern European civilization.

3. Assess the merits of Augustine's argument that Rome fell to the barbarians for religious rather than for political, economic, or social reasons.

4. Explain the differences between Augustine and Aquinas's epistemological approaches. What influences would these approaches have on later Protestant and Catholic thinkers?

5. Viewing modernity as a cultural and intellectual era, what are modernity's most important characteristics?

6. In your estimation, is the role of religion increasing or decreasing in Western society? Explain your answer.

7. (a) In your estimation, how do revelation and reason relate? Explain your answer. (b) From a moral perspective, why did Kant think that humans are obligated to believe in God?

8. What are the primary differences between Enlightenment approaches to religion and Schleiermacher's approach?

9. Explain Hegel's influence on nineteenth-century approaches to scripture.

7

Postmodern Spirituality

KANT, SCHLEIERMACHER, AND HEGEL offered influential models for thinking about religion and Christianity in modern terms, especially with reference to modern conceptions of reason, experience, ethics, and history. Equally influential, though not immediately, was Søren Kierkegaard's (1813–1855) Christian challenge to modernity. Kierkegaard, it appears, offers a bridge from modernism to postmodernism. While most thinkers argue that postmodern views of religion began in the late twentieth century, some view the turning point to lie with Kierkegaard, who defended religious truth, appealing not to rationality or to objectivity but rather to nonrational methodology or phenomena.

Faith, for Kierkegaard, is based upon passionate (heartfelt) affirmation of the divine, rather than upon rational or intellectual argumentation or proof. Likewise, he viewed revelation to be subjective in nature, potentially contrary to reason. Criticizing Hegel's world-historical effort to grasp Christian faith conceptually, Kierkegaard attacked modern efforts to make Christianity "reasonable." He emphasized the existential nature of faith, the idea that faith is only realized in the passionate commitment of the existing, not just the thinking, individual. In *Fear and Trembling* (1843), Kierkegaard presents the biblical story of Abraham's near-sacrifice of Isaac, viewing it as a paradigm of faith grounded in a passionate relation to God that defies clear explanation.

Kierkegaard disagreed with most of his contemporaries in disputing that ultimate truth—what we might call religious truth—is something humans can access through reason or experience. For most of Kierkegaard's contemporaries, religious truth is a human endeavor, something humans basically contain in themselves or can somehow realize by themselves. Kierkegaard explored a different approach—that ultimate truth is a gift and that it comes to us from a transcendent source. Even the capacity for receiving truth and for recognizing it in the first place is a gift. For Kierkegaard, humans were created for communion with the truth—with God—but humans lost this gift through sin. Salvation—the ability to recognize and overcome sin—is only available to human beings through Jesus. Even the ability to recognize sin and to accept God's gracious forgiveness are divine gifts. As Kierkegaard sees it, human reason takes "offense" at what he calls the "paradox" of faith. Faith, for Kierkegaard, is a kind of falling in love with Jesus Christ. It is not controlled by reason or will, but is like a gift one receives. Encounter with God through transformative love makes it possible for us to take a "leap of faith," and thus to "encounter" Jesus and receive the paradox not as something rational, but rather simply as paradox. For Kierkegaard, Jesus is the divine teacher who enables us to grasp God's gift. Kierkegaard makes it clear that Jesus is no ordinary teacher, but the only mediator of divine truth. It is an encounter with this teacher and not any other teacher or teaching that grants us awareness of sin and creates receptivity of transformative salvation. In this way, Kierkegaard rejected the significance of the historical study of Jesus and the gospels.

Kierkegaard's existential approach raises numerous questions. What does faith mean in this context? Is it "blind," or irrational? In this setting, can appeals to revelation be taken seriously or rationally, or must they be relegated to other realms or categories, such as mystery or fantasy? Do appeals to revelation involve being "close-minded," that is, closed to reason, argumentation, and common sense, or do they involve being truly "open-minded," open to intuition, imagination, inspiration, and other means of knowing and living? Furthermore, is such "open-mindedness" groundbreaking, that is, does it invoke a way of knowing accessible to the bold and courageous, a way of seeing that lies beyond the common and obvious ways of perception, a way of affirming that exceeds legitimating what is already known? Is religion a form of experimentation in harmony with science yet exceeding its limitations? Can human beings be religious by looking primarily forward and beyond, or must religious individuals be limited to what is primarily behind and affirmed? Must religious people know only as insiders, or can they be insiders and outsiders simultaneously? In other words, must people be nontraditionally religious to be postmodernly religious?

However viewed, one thing we sense repeatedly is that religious thought must be more than mindless and repetitive creedal affirmation; it can and often has been self-correcting and self-critical, as we have noted. While religious belief, however rationally justified, will likely never be universally accepted, for many religious philosophers and theologians, faith must take itself through the trial of suspicion, and such critical thinking is the one mark of rationality that brings religion as close to universal as it can get.

The Masters of Suspicion

In his essay "The Critique of Religion," French philosopher Paul Ricoeur (1913–2005) speaks of Marx, Nietzsche, and Freud as the "masters of suspicion." Unlike medieval and Reformation theologians, who placed great trust in the Bible and Christian theology, and unlike modern philosophers, who placed great trust in the clarity and transparency of human consciousness, the masters of suspicion questioned human consciousness altogether, rejecting the autonomy and transparency of consciousness and, thus, the ability of consciousness to clarify and correct itself. Ricoeur summarized Marx, Nietzsche, and Freud as follows:

1. For Karl Marx (1818–1883), consciousness, including religious ideology, conceals the social origins of alienation and domination.

2. For Friedrich Nietzsche (1844–1900), consciousness, including religious ideology, conceals struggles for power over self, others, and life itself.

3. For Sigmund Freud (1856–1939), consciousness, including religious ideology, is shaped by conflicts at the heart of psychic life, particularly repressed desire and wish fulfillment.

Each of these thinkers saw religion as a product of false consciousness. Rooting the phenomenon of religion in the human psyche, they felt it was not enough to dismiss religion as a mistake. Instead, it is necessary to diagnose religion, to understand it and thus interpret it as a symptom of fundamental conflicts and conditions human beings cannot face.

While these three thinkers employed the hermeneutics of suspicion[1] from an atheistic perspective, Ricoeur wishes to employ their tactics as

---

1. The term "hermeneutic" refers to a system or methodology of interpreting a concept, a perspective, or a text. The key feature of a hermeneutic of suspicion is that it takes

a form of "purification" of religion. In other words, mature faith cannot be based on fantasy and the desire to escape from reality. Such faith must incorporate in some way a hermeneutic of suspicion. The masters of suspicion show us the importance of confronting our "will to power," our economic exploitation, and the reality of our hidden desires, demonstrating how these can work to distort our religious lives. So mature faith must help us confront and defeat our "religious atheism," that is, our overt and covert idols, in order to create space where we can hear a more primal language, which, though addressed to us, we no longer hear.

Influenced by the twentieth century theologians Karl Barth (1886–1968) and Rudolf Bultmann (1884–1976), Ricoeur focuses on ways by which we might enhance spiritual receptivity to God's Word. He uses the concept of demythologization, finding ways to set aside historical and cultural concerns about the historical Jesus and about what is factual in the Bible, in order to encounter the living Christ through scripture and church worship. For Ricoeur, demythologization means translating the Bible into ways that make sense today, and thus, to encounter the timeless or core teachings of the Bible rather than its superficial cultural overlay.

This task, however, requires that we direct the hermeneutic of suspicion toward ourselves and our personal values, asking why it is that things make sense to us today. In this regard, we need to be suspicious of our own culture, Ricoeur argues, with its distinct values, including modern and postmodern assertions of human autonomy. Why, for instance, do modern people place hope in material possessions or economic success, and trust in cultural supremacy or on reason? Why are we driven by dominance and control over others, ourselves, and our planet? In this regard, Ricoeur calls us to explore our imagination, using this facility to experience the world in new ways. For example, literature such as poetry, myth, and epic can be revelatory, helping us to see ourselves in new ways. Thus, we must learn to apply poetic creativity to our reading of scripture and to our theological thought. This, for Ricoeur, is the power of revelation, that it opens our imagination to the new world of the gospel, to that reality we call the "kingdom of God." This task of opening believers to what Ricoeur calls "the grace of imagination" in revelation, is what distinguishes the theistic from the atheistic masters of suspicion. While Ricoeur focuses on special revelation (through scripture), he remains open to the possibility of general revelation

---

the meaning of religion to be hidden from the consciousness of individual believers.

(through history and in nature) as well, for, like an effective Lover, God uses any and all means to connect with the Beloved.

Other scholars, including "liberation theologians," "Black theologians," and "feminist theologians," direct the "hermeneutics of suspicion" against both secular and religious sources of domination and oppression, applying their concerns not only to dominant theological perspectives and religious institutions, but also to the church's complicity in oppressive systems of sexism, racism, and economic exploitation. The Latin American version of liberation theology is shaped by the long history of colonization in that region and by the wide gap between the rich and the poor that it produced. It criticizes the complicity of the church in the oppression. For example, El Salvador's martyred Catholic archbishop, Oscar Romero, spoke of the "beautiful but harsh truth that the Christian faith does not cut Christians off from the world but immerses them in it" as key for thinking about the way liberation theologians seek to reimagine the task of religious thought.

In his analysis of the masters of suspicion, Ricoeur seeks to decode "false consciousness," looking for thinkers that could destroy idols in order to create space where human beings might hear God's Word and engage with God's Will in ways undiluted by human activity. In so doing, he shows how such an approach to religion could deepen "the language of faith" by understanding it as symbolic language that opens up new possibilities for human existence.

Nietzsche's Dance with Nihilism

Postmodernism is not a rejection of modernity but refers to a complex and ambivalent attitude toward modernity grounded in a hermeneutics of suspicion directed at some of modernity's foundational ideas. In *The Gay Science*, sometimes translated as *The Joyful Wisdom* or *The Joyous Science*, published in 1882, Nietzsche criticized religion by arguing that God had died and was no longer relevant.

Let's be clear. For Nietzsche, God had not died literally. Saying that "God is dead" meant that the Christian God was no longer believable. The death of God, however, was not Nietshe's main point. The real news is that "we have killed him," meaning that modernity had made God irrelevant. The challenge is, are we ready to live with what we have done, that is, to remove all traces of Christian piety from society? In place of religious "slave morality"—timid, anxious, ascetic, and pessimistic—Nietzsche was interested in the possibility of a "gay science," by which he meant ways of living and thinking that were bold, dancelike, experimental, expansive, and daring; self-affirming rather than self-denying, life affirming rather than life-denying.

Closely connecting the death of God with a loss of meaning, the question of how we live after the death of God became crucial for him. His critique of religion also made him suspicious of modernity, including almost everything human beings find valuable and meaningful, including truth and morality. Like Kierkegaard, Nietzsche criticized modernity from an "existentialist" perspective that, unlike the traditionalists or fundamentalists, looked ahead to something beyond modernity.

Nietzsche claimed that for life to have meaning, our wills must have a goal. Affirming the death of God, Nietzsche wonders whether it is possible to find another meaning, another ideal or goal for the will. Nietzsche never directly answers the question of the alternative to religion. He suggests that we may not be in a position yet to answer the question of meaning, but acknowledges that the only real meaning to be found in life is precisely through immersion in this predicament. In *The Gay Science*, Nietzsche goes into more detail about the ways in which immersion in the problem of truth might be meaningful. He introduces the idea of the "free spirit," contrasting one kind of faith, the "wish for certainty," with another, a faith that allows him to dance near, without plunging into, the abyss of nihilism. This is faith not in another life, not in progress toward a utopia, but in the affirmation of life in all its strange, confusing, and painful reality.

Unlike Platonic and theistic solutions, the goal of life is not to escape this world, this Platonic "cave," with all its suffering and delusion. All humans have is the "cave," and we must learn to embrace it and make the best of it, motivated by what Nietzsche calls the "will to power"—in this case, the will to overcome our sick or guilty conscience. Two approaches, he suggests, enable us to embrace life fully; first, by exploring life with a suspicious eye toward all denials of life, and then by pursuing a kind of creative, artistic effort to make life beautiful. For Nietzsche, the death of God is not primarily about the end of religion but about the beginning of nihilism, a state in which one's life has no overarching goal, orientation, or direction. Nietzsche distinguished two forms of nihilism, the state in which our will wills nothing, and the state of traditional religion, in which people aim at God and goodness, which ultimately are delusions, what Nietzsche called forms of "willing nothingness," and theists call idolatry, meaning false worship or adoration.[2]

Martin Heidegger (1889–1976), the German philosopher widely regarded as one of the most important philosophers of the twentieth century, is most readily associated with phenomenology and existentialism. Exploring the meaning of Nietzsche's death of God, Heidegger argued that it should be understood, not as an actual death of a being that was once alive but has died due to age or neglect, but as the death of metaphysics, the death of a certain way of thinking and doing philosophy.

Bonhoeffer's Call for "Religionless Christianity"

Following the challenges of modern thinkers, including the radical critiques of the "masters of suspicion," the growing secularization of the "first world" in the latter half of the twentieth century further challenged religious thought. The "death of God" movement responded to secular suspicions of religious other-worldliness by embracing secularization. A major influence on these theologies was the German theologian Dietrich Bonhoeffer's call for a "religionless Christianity."

Bonhoeffer (1906–1945), a pastor and theologian who studied under Barth and Bultmann, was arrested and executed by the Nazis for participating in plots against Hitler. Unlike Barth, who stressed the "otherness" of God, Bonhoeffer focused on the unity of God and humanity through Jesus Christ in the church. This idea was explored in his early writings, but it took a sharp turn in his letters from prison. In these writings, Bonhoeffer focuses less on the church as the place of encounter with God and more on how this union is to be found in the secular world. Disdaining religiosity as something superficial and unchristian, Bonhoeffer writes to his friend Eberhard Bethge,

> You would be surprised, and perhaps even worried, by my theological thoughts and [to] the conclusions that they lead . . . What is bothering me incessantly is the question what Christianity really is, or indeed who Christ really is, for us today . . . We are moving

2. In his letters from prison, Dietrich Bonhoeffer notes his disagreement with the usual interpretation of idolatry as "wealth, sensuality, and pride," finding such emphasis unbiblical and merely moralizing. "Idols are things we worship, and idolatry implies that people still worship something." However, according to Bonhoeffer, people nowadays don't worship anything, not even idols. "In that regard," he adds, agreeing with Nietzsche, "we're truly nihilists." *Letters & Papers*, 336.

towards a completely religionless time; people as they are now simply cannot be religious any more. Even those who honestly describe themselves as "religious" do not in the least act up to it, and so they presumably mean something quite different by "religious"... What do a church, a community, a sermon, a liturgy, a Christian life mean in a religionless world?... How do we speak in a "secular" way about "God"?[3]

Later he writes, "To be a Christian does not mean to be religious in a particular way... It is not the religious act that makes the Christian, but participation in the sufferings of God in the secular world."[4] Bonhoeffer felt that seeking Christ privately, apart from the world, or exclusively through the church were both ways of avoiding the cost of discipleship.

He wrote about modernity as a "world come of age," in which "before God and with God we live without God." In other words, we should come to see modernity not as threatening our unity with God, but as a new, more mature stage of this unity. For Bonhoeffer, "The world that has come of age is more godless, and perhaps for that very reason nearer to God, than the world before its coming of age."[5] This meant that the criticisms of religion found in Marx, Nietzsche, and Freud should be taken seriously, not as blanket condemnations of Christianity, but as ways of understanding that organized religion represents a kind of immature stage of the relation between God and humans.

What became crucial for Bonhoeffer was not the religious form of faith in God and Christ, but faith as discipleship, as following Christ in his work in the world. From this perspective, the point is not to develop theories of God, or cultivate inner spirituality, but to engage others and the world in a Christlike way. At least in some way, this meant, for Bonhoeffer, that we should learn "before and with God to live without God." By so doing, we meet God at the cross, meaning through vulnerability and suffering, rather than in the comfort and convenience of "life as usual." In this respect, it is no surprise that Bonhoeffer has had a powerful effect on liberation theology as well as the "death of God" and "secular theology" movement. His death as a martyr prevented him from conceptualizing further the implications of his hypothesis, but a religionless—perhaps even a nontheistic or godless—Christianity appeared on the horizon of his thinking.

---

3. Bonhoeffer, *Letters & Papers*, 279–80.
4. Bonhoeffer, *Letters & Papers*, 361.
5. Bonhoeffer, *Letters & Papers*, 362.

The Church Alumni Association

Bonhoeffer's writings gained fame and credibility because of his remarkable life. Despite a short life, ended tragically and prematurely at age thirty-nine, Bonhoeffer remains an influential thinker today, inspiring theologians and Christians of widely different persuasions. To a great extent, the influence of Bonhoeffer is based on his life. Active in the ecumenical life of global Christianity, he was one of the first Germans to detect the evil of Nazism. Because of his outspoken criticism of Hitler's regime, he often had to work underground. For a time he was in charge of an illegal seminary, speaking of the strength he gathered from worship in *Life Together*. He left Germany for brief periods, including a time when he was pastor of an English congregation. In 1939, just prior to World War II, he was visiting in the United States. His friends urged him to stay, but he felt he could only participate in the postwar rebuilding of Germany if he had been there through the dark years, so he returned home. While there, he became involved in the underground resistance movement against Nazism, even joining a group that plotted Hitler's death. He was arrested in 1943 and spent two years in prison before his execution on April 9, 1945, just weeks before American troops arrived to liberate his area.

While in prison, Bonhoeffer won the respect of his inmates and guards. The latter allowed him to smuggle out letters to Bethge, published eventually under the title *Letters & Papers from Prison*. He died as he lived, witnessing to his faith. As guards came to take him to his death, he said quietly to an inmate, "This is the end. For me the beginning of life."

A major problem in interpreting Bonhoeffer is deciding what is significant in his letters. Personal in nature, they were never intended for publication. Do they indicate a new direction in his thinking, or should they be understood as extensions of his earlier ideas? Based on such striking phrases as "the world has come of age" and has grown "beyond religion," some scholars argue that Bonhoeffer was moving away from Christianity. Others argue that he had come to see that in order for Christianity to survive in the modern world, it must be restructured. Of course, we will never know precisely what he felt or envisioned about his faith. Perhaps the most we can say is that he was "a creative and dynamic thinker who was continually developing his thought."[6]

Bonhoeffer focused on ethics in his last major work, left incomplete and published posthumously. In *Ethics* (1949) we find many of the themes in the prison letters, often more fully developed than in his letters.

---

6. Hordern, *Layman's Guide to Protestant Theology*, 213.

Bonhoeffer had a gift for putting his thought into striking phrases, such as "cheap grace" and "costly grace." These concepts, developed in his classic work, *The Cost of Discipleship* (1937), challenged Protestant churches in general and his own Lutheran church in particular with the costly price tag of grace, costly for God and for Jesus and his followers. His book was a call for a radical discipleship that confronts not only secular culture but all forms of Christianity that fail to challenge Christians with the true meaning of discipleship: "When Christ calls a man," he wrote, "He bids him come and die." For Bonhoeffer, the cross is the true measure of discipleship and ethics, for to hear the call of Jesus is to hear the command to follow the crucified and risen Christ in suffering, rejection, and even in death. At the height of World War II, Bonhoeffer was already looking ahead to the postwar world, where he saw that people would need new ways of thinking about their society.

In speaking of society "come of age" and of "religionless Chritianity," Bonhoeffer was combatting the popular assumption that humans are religious by nature, or that the religious aspirations of humanity find their most adequate fulfillment in Christianity. This is what Schleiermacher had done by beginning with the universal religious feeling within humans, and arguing from this to the superiority of Christianity. Bonhoeffer also singled out Paul Tillich[7] as an example of approaching unbelievers on the assumption that they are already religious. If we are to understand Bonhoeffer's call for religionless Christianity, we need to understand what he meant by "religion."

Bonhoeffer disdained the word "religion" because of its inherent dualism, that is, as a perspective that divides life and the world into competing spheres, sacred and secular, or holy and profane. Life, for a "religious" person, is the place of tension and conflict between the demands of the sacred and the profane. Religions see certain individuals, professions, acts, and books as sacred and the rest as profane. Religion values the sacred and devalues the profane. Like Luther, Bonhoeffer fought this division, arguing for a unitive consciousness. In speaking of costly grace, Bonhoeffer had in mind serving Christ in the world. Rather than separating from society, Christians must be in the world, working in all phases of society to remind humanity that God loves the word, not a world fractured by religion, but united and loved by grace.

---

7. For information on Paul Tillich, see the discussion in chapter 8 below.

The Church Alumni Association

Religion has disappeared, Bonhoeffer argued, because humanity has "come of age." The modern world answers all questions and solves all problems without reference to God. It seems, Bonhoeffer states, that God has willfully accepted being edged out of the world and on to a cross because it is not through omnipotence that God saves the world, but rather through weakness. Thus the world, come of age, has cleared the decks for the incarnated, crucified God of the Bible. Jesus offers the opposite of what "religious" humans expect. The biblical God is not calling disciples away from the world and into purely sacred realms and endeavors, but rather is calling us to plunge into the religionless world and share the sufferings of God. In denying the sacred-secular distinctions of religion, Bonhoeffer is also rejecting the inward-outward and individual-social dichotomies of religion. The Old Testament, Bonhoeffer argued, shows no interest in personal or individual salvation and, properly understood, neither does the New Testament.

By "religionless Christianity," Bonhoeffer did not mean to imply that Christians should abandon the church or quit praying and worshiping. However, through his life, he attacked the idea that there are any spheres that do not belong to God. As Christ cannot be confined to the "sacred" society of the church, so Christians should not confine themselves to "sacred" activities or to "inner" spirituality as though it were the sole source and repository of their spiritual talents or resources. The Bible sees humans as a totality, and it is our wholeness that is claimed by God. Thus, the place for the church is not on a hill far away, but at the center of society, not on the borders of life but in the factories, laboratories, and marketplaces of life.

We do not know how Bonhoeffer would have developed his thought had he lived a longer life, but one concept we must examine is his reference to God as being not on the boundaries of life but as "the Beyond in the midst of life." While reaffirming the traditional view that God is both immanent and transcendent, Bonhoeffer emphasized that God is to be found in what we know, not in what we do not know. Often we relegate God to the "gaps" of life, to the realm of mystery or the unknown. However, when we do this, we reduce God, making God too small rather than too large, limiting God to the level of things we already known, only greater. We call God the First Cause because everything needs a cause. However, despite our references to "bigger and better," God has simply become another cog in the wheel, another number in a series. As such, God is no longer the "Beyond."

If God is the Beyond "in the midst of life," we acknowledge that God is in the processes we know, working through them, yet in a manner and dimension different from them. In Bonhoeffer's sense, God is to be found, "not in a few exotic experiences or situations, but as a dimension in the whole of life."[8] Therefore, Christians are called to plunge fully into the life of this world, not to fall into the shallows of life, the kind of worldliness characterized by the convenient, the busy, the comfortable, or the salacious, and there remain. Faith requires far more, including acquaintance with death and resurrection. To be "in Christ," for Bonhoeffer, is to live fully in the moment, for it is only by living fully in the world that we learn to believe.

Vattimo's "Secular Theology"

The term "secular theology" might sound like an oxymoron, but it has been a significant movement in European and North American Christian theological circles since the middle of the twentieth century. Secular means "worldly," and many see the process called secularization—a process in which religion plays a diminishing role in society—as central to what we are calling modernity. This transformation has occurred in various ways, including in the separation of church and state, and more recently, in the significant decrease in the number of people who consider themselves religious or who regularly attend church worship. We also see the privatization and individualization of religion and note that these trends mean less influence of organized religion on public life.

Bonhoeffer's thought led in various directions, but one such direction was that taken up by the Italian philosopher Gianni Vattimo (born 1936), who describes his book *Belief* as an effort to treat secularization as "the constitutive trait of an authentic religious experience." Vattimo and other contemporary theologians have been influenced by philosophical postmodernism, particularly by Nietzsche and Heidegger. Vattimo appropriates the postmodernism that comes out of Nietzsche and Heidegger by describing secularization as a "purification" of Christianity. God's revelation, according to Vattimo, is a revelation of love that Christians are to embody in the world. Vattimo views secularization not as a threat to religion but as the end of the otherworldly "metaphysics" that characterizes traditional religion. Echoing Hegel, he reads the incarnation of Christ as marking the

---

8. Hordern, *Layman's Guide to Protestant Theology*, 229.

end of such otherworldliness, and understands divine transcendence as the emptying of divine love into the world.

Vattimo argues that from the beginning religion was an essentially interpretive discourse, proceeding by endlessly deconstructing its own sacred texts, so that from the start it had the potential to liberate itself from metaphysical orthodoxy. In opposition to the Enlightenment view, which envisioned freedom as lying in the perfect knowledge of and conformity to the structure of reality, Vattimo substitutes an appreciation of multiple discourses and the contingency and finitude of all religious, ethical, and political values—including our own. He wants to bring down "walls," including the walls that separate theists and atheists; the ideal society should be based on charity rather than truth.

Religion, as described by postmodern philosophers, may sound alien to much "modern" religion, but it evokes many of the insights of the past. Vattimo's claim that religion is essentially interpretive recalls the maxim of the rabbis: "What is Torah? It is the interpretation of Torah." When Vattimo affirms the primacy of charity and the communal nature of religious truth, we recall the rabbis' insistence that "when two or three study Torah together, the Shekinah [the immanence of God] is in their midst." This is also the story of Emmaus and the communal experience of liturgy.

Like Vattimo, the American philosopher John D. Caputo stresses the importance of the apophatic, arguing that atheists and theists alike should abandon the modern appetite for certainty. Such perceptions, once central to religion, tended to be submerged during modernity, and the fact that they have surfaced again in a different form suggests that this type of unknowing is inherent in our humanity. The distinctively modern yearning for absolute and empirically proven truth is most likely an aberration. Noting that atheism is always a rejection of a particular conception of the divine, Caputo concludes: "If modern atheism is the rejection of a modern God, then the delimitation of modernity opens up another possibility, less the resuscitation of premodern theism than the chance of something beyond both the theism and the atheism of modernity."[9]

This raises a tantalizing possibility. If, as Caputo argues, we are entering a "postmodern" phase, is it possible that modern atheism will, like modern theism, become obsolete? Will the growing appreciation of the limitations of human knowledge—which is just as much a part of the

---

9. Caputo, "Atheism, A/theology," 283.

contemporary intellectual scene as atheistic certainty—give rise to a new kind of apophatic understanding of theology?

A common criticism of postmodernism is that it is a destructive relativism that only takes things apart, deconstructive of tradition rather than reconstructive. This criticism has made room for what we might call postmodern traditionalism, an approach found in the work of the Jewish thinker Emmanuel Levinas, a philosopher who was born in Lithuania but spent most of his life teaching in Paris. Influenced by Heidegger, Levinas argues that ethics should not be subordinated to metaphysics or epistemology, but rather should be based on the "experience of obligation" for "the other," a transcendent imperative central to all human relationship. For Levinas, it is in the ethical relationship with "the other" and with "otherness," particularly with the suffering of "the other," that we are freed from our human narcissism. This is the way of self-surrender, of divine kenosis;[10] through "surrender to divine justice," we find ourselves related to God. Ultimately, it is faith that allows us to live, make decisions, find meaning, and act morally. Levinas helps us to find a faith freed from the modern distinction between the secular and the religious, a faith freed, you might say, both from metaphysics and from dogma.

Postmodernism as a Way of Unknowing

Philosophy and theology have always responded to the science of the day, and postmodernism is both a philosophical and a theological movement that embraces the indeterminacy of the new physics. Postmodernism is a way of thinking that builds on the assumption that what we call reality is constructed by the mind, and that human understanding is interpretation rather than acquisition of accurate, objective information. From this it follows that our knowledge is relative, subjective, and fallible rather than certain and absolute, and that truth is inherently ambiguous.

Postmodernism is iconoclastic. Inherited ideas are the products of a particular historical and cultural milieu, including the modern emphasis on reason and science as paths to peace, certainty, and a better future, and therefore are to be deconstructed. Since this analysis is not based on any absolute principle, there is no assurance that we can ever arrive at a wholly accurate version of truth. Fundamental to postmodern thought is the conviction that

---

10. The kenosis of Jesus (that is, his self-emptying) is found in Paul's "kenotic hymn" in Philippians 2:6–11.

sense data cannot force us to adopt a particular worldview, so we have a choice in what we affirm—as well as an immense responsibility.

While postmodernism is suspicious of Big Stories—whether theological, scientific, economic, ideological, or political—it is also averse to an atheism that makes absolute, totalistic claims. As Jacques Derrida (1930–2004) cautioned, we must be alert to "theological prejudices," not only in religious contexts, where they are overt, but in all metaphysics—even those that profess to be atheist. Derrida, a secularized Jew, had a messianic hope for a better world and inclined to the view that, since no absolute certainty is within our grasp, for the sake of peace, we should hesitate to make declarative statements of either belief or unbelief. While some religious believers are repelled by such unabashed relativism, there are aspects of Derrida's thought that recall earlier theological attitudes. His theory of deconstruction, which denies the possibility of finding a single, secure meaning in any text, is rabbinical. He has also been called a "negative" theologian, for he was greatly interested in Meister Eckhart, the medieval apophatic mystic.

While today we still find many defenders of the secularization thesis, who view secularization either as inevitable or at least as an ideal toward which America must strive, others argue that secularization is faulty or invalid, and that the resurgence of public religion indicates that modernity is over and that we have entered a postmodern phase of American history, a time of new thinking about the role of religion in public and private life. The spectrum of possibilities is extensive, ranging from "death of God" thinking to increased emphasis on faith and the validity of divine revelation.

One response to the reemergence of religion around the world today is what some are calling the "new atheism," a group of scholars and thinkers who argue that for the sake of human survival, we must eliminate religion altogether. Among these detractors, some of the more significant include Richard Dawkins, Daniel Dennett, Sam Harris, and Christopher Hitchens. In their writings, these authors argue that religion is inherently irrational and intolerant, and that it is a leading factor in much of the world's conflicts and violence today. Viewing religious fundamentalism, with its extreme scriptural literalism and intolerance, as not only the most dangerous form of religion but also as the truest and most authentic form of religion, these writers exhort people of good will everywhere to work for the end of organized and particularly of politicized religion. Only thus, they argue, can humanity survive. Surprisingly, such thinkers are also critical of religious moderates—namely, of those who think that one can be both religious and modern simultaneously—whom they oppose on two grounds.

First, they view such moderates as not truly religious but rather as misguided or ignorant of the modern sensibility. Furthermore, they view religious moderates as dangerous, because they are said to mislead themselves and others into thinking that religion can be moderate and hence tolerant by nature. For new atheists, religious faith is incompatible with reason. Such faith is unable to evolve, they maintain, for they view all traditional religious traditions as opposed to debate or to new learning. In their estimation, one is either religious and irrational or irreligious and rational. There is no third option.

However, as most of us are aware, there are other options, for many people today join a host of believers over the past several centuries who considered themselves both modern and religious, rational and spiritual. Believing that religious faith need not be blind or uncritical, they read their scriptures metaphorically rather than literally. For them, religion can be rational, pluralistic, compassionate, and nonviolent, meaning that religion can uphold an intellectually viable and realistic view of reality.

For many today, however, modernity has outlived its usefulness and persuasiveness. They claim that we have entered a postmodern age, a way of thinking that builds on the assumption that what we call reality is constructed by the mind, and that human understanding is interpretation rather than acquisition of objective information. From this it follows that all human knowledge is relative, subjective, and fallible rather than certain and absolute, and that truth is inherently ambiguous. Assertions about reason, progress, and universality, said to be characteristic of modernity, must be deconstructed, for they are viewed as misguided, too limited and oblivious to the fundamental differences between humans, cultures, and even between notions of progress, reason, and truth. Significantly, this turn to postmodernism changes how religion is regarded.

For some postmodern thinkers, there really is no such thing as pluralism, whereby one "truth" fits all, and even what we call pluralism is a form of disguised exclusivism. For other postmodern thinkers, the best answer to religious diversity is neither exclusivism, inclusivism, or pluralism, but rather one or another form of secularism. Accepting the general framework of modernity, the state, they argue, should remain separate from religion, and the secular state should guarantee the politics of liberation, that is, a politics of liberty and the pursuit of happiness. Secularism is the ideal for modernists and postmodernists alike, for it seeks to create a context in which people from all faiths and even with no religious faith can debate and engage on a level playing field.

There are multiple types of fundamentalism in our world today, some religious, others political, and others scientific. Typical of the fundamentalist mindset is the belief that there is only one way of interpreting reality. For the new atheists, scientism alone can lead us to truth. However, science depends upon faith, intuition, and aesthetic vision as well as on reason. As theologian Paul Tillich pointed out, men and women continually feel drawn to explore levels of truth that go beyond normal experience. This imperative, called an "ultimate concern" by Tillich, inspired the scientific as well as the religious quest and continues to shape life and give it meaning. The ultimate concern of new atheists such as Dawkins and Harris appears to be reason. However, their idea of reason is very different from the rationality of Socrates, who used his reasoning powers to bring his dialogue partners into a state of unknowing, or the rationality of Augustine and Aquinas, for whom reason became *intellectus*, opening naturally to the divine. Reason, for many people today, rules supreme and is the only way to truth. The danger of this secularization of reason, which denies the possibility of transcendence, is that reason can become an idol that seeks to destroy all rival claimants.

As anthropologist Ian Tattersall notes in his superb book, *Becoming Human*, science fiction writers who created the character of Spock in the *Star Trek* series "hit close to home when they invented that supremely rational being. For there is undeniably something bizarrely seductive in the notion of living unencumbered by all the emotional baggage that being human inevitably entails. After all, irrational behavior, propelled by obscure emotion, has lain behind most of the endless misery that the human species has inflicted on itself (and others) over the course of recorded history. Yet there's a flip side to this, of course, for none of us would wish to be an automaton, and a life without emotion would be a life without exhilaration, love, and joy."[11]

---

11. Tattersall, *Becoming Human*, 239–40.

Postmodern Spirituality

Questions for Discussion and Reflection

1. Explain Kierkegaard's "existentialist" approach to the theological task, and how he represents a departure from the majority of modern philosophers and theologians.
2. In what respects is faith a "passion" for Kierkegaard?
3. How would you distinguish the hermeneutics of suspicion from Enlightenment questions about religion? How does Ricoeur seek to integrate suspicion into the theological task?
4. Explain why Bonhoeffer's writings have influenced Christian thinkers across the theological spectrum, from modern to postmodern, conservative to liberal.
5. What did Nietzsche mean by "nihilism"?
6. In your estimation, what did Nietzsche mean by the "death of God"?
7. Explain and assess Gianni Vattimo's understanding of the relation of secularization and Christianity?
8. Assess the merits of the "new atheists" critique of religion. In your estimation, is religion inherently intolerant of diversity, as the "new atheists" claim?

8

Rethinking Revelation

IMPORTANT TO ANY SYSTEM of knowledge is its starting point. In most cases, this starting point is a presupposition, something unprovable and yet necessary to that system. This holds true for all disciplines, including science, economics, sociology, politics, even philosophy and religion. All monotheistic religions begin with common presuppositions, with two basic assumptions about God, namely, that God exists, and that God communicates. Such assumptions bring us to the concept of revelation, taken from the Greek word *apokalypsis*, from which we get the related word "apocalypse." Both words have the basic meaning of "removing a veil so that something new can be seen or understood." The key here is that in order to reveal something new, the old must be displaced or removed.

The concept of revelation is central to Christianity, as it is to all monotheistic religions. In an attempt to shed light on the various elements of this idea, Christian theologians have distinguished between two forms of God's self-revelation: general revelation, available to all people, and special revelation, given to humans in unique historical events such as the incarnation and resurrection. Besides Christ, the living Word of God, God's special self-revelation occurs through scripture, which interprets and clarifies revelatory events in history, giving them meaning.

As its name implies, general revelation is available to all humans regardless of time, place, culture, or other historical factors. General revelation is non-verbal. It is God's self-disclosure in nature, the human mind (or conscience), and through the events of history. The purpose of general revelation is clear: all humans live in nature (viewed as God's created order) and in history, and through such experience humans can know God and gain insight into the qualities that give meaning and purpose to life. According to the Bible, if humans were not sinful, general revelation would be sufficient for them to know God accurately and relate to God authentically. However, as Paul indicates in Romans 1, sinfulness leads humans to "suppress the truth," distorting the truth about God's sovereignty, providence, and standards, resulting not only in ignorance but also in idolatry and autonomy.

In a Christian context, theologians draw a distinction between "knowing about God" and "knowing God." While it is common to reduce revelation to doctrine, that is, to the transmission of a body of knowledge, in a deeper sense, revelation also involves communication or impartation of the personal presence or self-disclosure of God, both externally, that is, through nature and history, but also internally, as a "living faith" or experience within individual believers.

Barth's Critique of Liberal Theology

At the start of the twentieth century, an influential movement emerged in Protestant Christianity known as neo-orthodoxy. The key figure in this movement was the Swiss theologian Karl Barth (1886–1968), considered the greatest Christian theologian of the twentieth century. In time, Barth became known for the manner in which he applied the theological concerns of Reformed Protestantism to the prevailing liberal theology. Barth gave his ideas systematic exposition in his *Church Dogmatics* (1930–1969), one of the most significant theological achievements of the twentieth century.

Neo-orthodoxy, sometimes called Religious Existentialism, had its roots in the existentialist thought of Kierkegaard, which initially profoundly influenced Barth. In the late 1920s, Barth began writing his *Dogmatics* and completed one large volume. When critics pointed out that it was dependent upon existentialist philosophy, Barth began over again. This became a decisive turning point in his theological development. Henceforth he determined to build his theology upon orthodox Christian thought, taking the incarnation of Christ as his starting point.

Twentieth-century religious thought really begins with the publication of Barth's *Epistle to the Romans* in the aftermath of World War I. Shaken by the brutality of the war, Barth rejected the close links between the gospel and modern Western culture asserted by liberal religious thinkers of the nineteenth century. Nineteenth-century Protestant liberals, it seems, stressed general revelation almost exclusively. Focusing on God's immanence rather than on God's transcendence, they limited revelation to what comes through nature, history, and the human mind, as well as to what is ideally exemplified in Jesus, who, though the exemplar of God's character, will, and nature, was merely mortal. Neo-orthodox thinkers such as Barth stressed God's transcendence, focusing on special revelation, though some, like Emil Brunner (1889–1966), argued that a fragment of general revelation remains available.

In 1918, as World War I was ending, Barth, then a pastor in a small Swiss town, published the first edition of his commentary on Romans, followed up by a second edition in 1922. His scathing attack on liberal theology in this book became a sensation. Before the war, Barth had studied under two of the most prominent liberal theologians, Adolf von Harnack and Wilhelm Herrmann, and he was disillusioned by the failure of his teachers to speak out against the war. Furthermore, he found their theology of little use as a pastor, so he spent the war years radically rethinking his approach to Christianity.

In 1921 Barth became a professor in Sweden, and in 1929 he relocated to Germany, where he taught at Bonn. He watched the rise of Hitler with concern and became one of the founders of the Confessional Church in Germany, which resisted attempts to unite Christianity with Nazism. In 1934 he helped to draft the famous Barmen Declaration, which repudiated Hitler's totalitarian dictatorship, declaring that the church's allegiance is to God alone. In 1935, refusing to take a loyalty oath to Nazism, he fled from Germany, accepting a professorship at the Swiss university in Basle, from which he retired in 1962.

Barth's approach to the Bible, Christianity, and theology ushered in a new paradigm for thinking about faith and suspicion, one that not only differed from the theologians in the liberal tradition, but also from the traditionalists and fundamentalists, who held a radically different approach to the biblical message and its interpretation. Initially, Barth called his approach "dialectical theology," referring to the give and take in an argument or conversation, especially in God's "No" and "Yes," because Barth was interested in the way in which God communicates with humans, first the negative and then the positive side of revelation.

It is by viewing religion as a place of encounter with God, but also as "unbelief" (that is, as a substitute for genuine encounter), that we see the "dialectical" nature of Barth's thinking. Humans can only talk theologically by shifting between these two perspectives, without allowing them to collapse into one another or to contradict one another. Theological talk values both poles, which appear as opposites, and tries to maintain the tension between them. We see a similar tension in Martin Luther, who maintained that Christians are simultaneously saints and sinners, fallen yet justified at the same time. Nevertheless, the gulf remains between humans and God, and the more we try to get to God on our own, whether through religious, philosophical, or ethical activity—the more we try to comprehend God or experience God through our own efforts—the more we sin (that is, he more we become caught in idolatry and "unbelief").

When Barth's biblical commentary appeared, it hit the public like a bombshell. Interestingly, Barth used the image of a bombshell regularly. Speaking of revelation as an "event" caused by God, Barth viewed God's communication with humanity the explosion. The crater left behind by the explosion of God's revelation is religion—the institutionalized Christian church, religious consciousness (so central to Schleiermacher's theological approach), and all other human religiosity. Revelation, for Barth, was an event through which God says both No and Yes to humanity, shaping the dialectic in Barth's theology.

Building his theological perspective, like Augustine, on the principle of "faith seeking understanding," Barth noted in his commentary on Romans that faith, which he defined as "knowledge of God," is an "impossible possibility." It is this idea of the distance of the human and the divine that Barth mentions repeatedly. On their own, knowledge of God is impossible for humans because human faith cannot reach God, but such knowledge becomes possible because God is able to reach humanity. Theology (faith), for Barth, is one-way communication, from God outward, and authentic faith must see things from God's point of view rather than from human perspective.

Barth faced what Kierkegaard must have faced in Denmark, a Christianity that accommodated with secularism. "If I have a system," Barth wrote, "it consists in what Kierkegaard called the infinite qualitative difference between time and eternity." For Barth, the starting point of theology must be God's transcendence, not any human ability or capacity for transcendence. This approach led to Barth's rejection of liberal values and perspectives such as the emphasis on human experience. For Barth, the event of revelation shatters human efforts and perspectives, and what it leaves behind (including human consciousness and awareness) is but the crater. Contrasting "religion" with "revelation," he viewed the task of Christian theology as one of "confession," by which he meant acknowledging and reflecting on God's saving message.

Eventually, Barth's perspective resonated with a diverse group of thinkers, all of whom gathered around his understanding of revelation as "existential event."

Barth was not an enemy of modernity as such, but he claimed that any theology that begins with religion as a human capacity falls into the modern tendency to emphasize human autonomy over God's authority and our status as God's creatures. Like Kierkegaard, Barth didn't want to defend religion per se, but rather wished to do theology from divine priority and activity.

For Barth, Schleiermacher and others had glorified the human at the expense of the divine. Emphasizing God's transcendence to all that is human, including religion, Barth agreed with religious critics such as Ludwig Feuerbach (1804–1872), who argued that theology is actually anthropology, for religion is just human beings talking about themselves. What we call "religion" is therefore a lie, or "unbelief."

Barth was convinced that if humans begin the religious task (the search for God) with religious experience, they end up turning that experience into God. In other words, if we begin with Schleiermacher, we end up with Feuerbach. By noting that the attitude of the antichristian masters of suspicion was more truly theological than that of many liberal theologians, Barth brings us to a crucial point in our thinking about faith, for he is telling us that suspicion of religion is not the sole task of the atheist, but is central to the biblical message and to the theological task.

We can think here of the biblical story of the Israelites fashioning a golden calf under Aaron's supervision at the same time as Moses is on Mount Sinai receiving the law from God. On the other hand, we can think about the prophet Amos, who says to Israel, "I hate, I despise your [religious] festivals, and I take no delight in your solemn assemblies" (Amos 5:21). For Barth, such stories should not be taken as examples of our tendency to doubt God, or as pointing to the difference in rituals between Catholics, Protestants, and Jews, but rather as a critique of all human religions.

For Barth, all human worship is idolatry. In this sense, Barth is as suspicious of religion as Marx, Nietzsche, and Freud. However, Barth sees such suspicion not as modern, but rather as thoroughly biblical. In this respect, Christians must be suspicious, not only of other religions, but of Christian religion as well. Unlike secular masters of suspicion, however, Barth did not remain in his critical perspective, but was able to move forward to develop

Rethinking Revelation

a constructive view of Christian theology, particularly in his view of revelation and biblical interpretation.

Barth and most neo-orthodox thinkers rejected modernity's project of defending Christian faith by means of rational or experiential arguments. By appealing to external or internal authorities, we acknowledge that humans can judge the divine, something we are in no position to do. However, like Kierkegaard, Barth maintained that God not only gives humans the revelation, but also the capacity to receive that revelation. This is not due to some human capability, but rather is a gift of God's Word, lost through sin, but restored by God. In this respect, humans are fully dependent upon God for truth and salvation.

While Barth and neo-orthodox thinkers in general focus on special rather than on general revelation, we must be careful to understand that Barth maintained that divine inspiration applies only to the *activity* of receiving revelation from God, and not to the *content* itself. Human words can never capture God's Word; hence, believers should not directly equate God's Word and the Bible. Since the Bible contains human words, it cannot be revelation per se, but only a witness to revelation. The role of the Bible is to point to Christ, to create space for God's self-revelation. According to Barth, the Bible is fallible—it contains errors, historical and scientific inaccuracies, and theological contradictions. Hence, we can subject the Bible to historical criticism. However, despite its fallibility, the Bible *can become* the Word of God, but only in those parts and at those times when God chooses to reveal Godself. Consequently, the Word of God is not something humans can possess, not something that resides permanently in the Bible, for the Word of God resides only with God. While Barth affirms that God was acting in events such as the incarnation and resurrection of Christ, he also notes that their deeper meaning remains elusive, something the original writers of scripture and later interpreters could not fully exhaust.

While the Bible can become a means of revelation, for Barth, revelation occurs only in Jesus Christ, and scripture is a witness, attesting to this revelation. However, although Christ is the primary form of revelation, there are actually three forms of the Word of God, (1) the written Word—scripture, (2) the preached Word—including proclamation and the sacraments, and (3) the revealed Word—Christ. Thus, scripture, preaching, and the sacraments may become the Word of God, but they only acquire this function as they reveal Christ. The first two forms—indirect witnesses—are primarily pointers to revelation.

The Church Alumni Association

Post-Barthian Theories of Revelation

It is safe to say that Barth's thought set the theological agenda for the twentieth century and beyond. After Barth, it became impossible to accept without reservation either Schleiermacher's starting point in experience and consciousness, or the nineteenth-century liberal assumptions between Christianity and culture. Barth challenged religious thinkers to take seriously the relativity, even the idolatry, of all human experiences and projects by emphasizing the transcendence or "otherness" of God, which condemns human religiosity.

However, criticisms of Barth emerged, primarily from those who argued that his views of God's transcendence did not adequately address the human experience of and response to revelation. The question became, "Are human beings completely passive in receiving revelation, or is there some form of active religious reception to revelation on their part?" For many, Barth's understanding of revelation was too objective, excluding any consideration of how humans receive revelation. Barth's emphasis on God's action left the question of the relation of Christianity to culture as vexed as ever. At some point, revelation must include a discussion of the questions, categories, and consciousness humans bring to their engagement with the divine.

In this segment, we address two very different Protestant approaches to this issue, the views of Paul Tillich, one of the most influential theologians of the mid-twentieth century, and the evangelical theologian Carl F. H. Henry, who even more than Barth, placed emphasis on the objectivity of divine revelation. Both of these approaches may be called theologies of "correlation," in that they focus on the relationship between human questions and Christian answers to them. Such approaches, like Barth's, have a confessional nature, in that they start with faith in God as the answer to the human predicament, but they are apologetic in the sense that they affirm the necessity of explaining how this answer makes sense in terms of the culture in which the question is raised and the answer is proclaimed. Hence, the apologetic task requires of the theologian careful analysis of the human pole of this equation, using the resources of philosophy and the social sciences to show how, in a given cultural context, human beings are asking questions that create space or an opening to God's revelation. For correlational theology, answers only make sense if they are given in response to questions people are asking.

Rethinking Revelation
Paul Tillich (1886-1965)

Arguably the most important correlational theologian of the twentieth century, Tillich in his early career followed Barth, convinced that Barth's emphasis on divine transcendence offered a crucial corrective to the liberal theology of the nineteenth century. In addition, like Barth, Tillich's political activities got him into trouble in the 1930s. Forced to flee Germany in 1933, he began an influential teaching career in the United States, first at Union Theological Seminary in New York City, and later at Harvard and at the University of Chicago. Speaking to both undergraduates and graduates, his classes were always packed, and his sermons, aimed at urban audiences, attracted overflow crowds, including many who considered themselves atheists, humanists, and secularists.

Tillich is called the "theologian's theologian." While his writings are never easy reading, he was completely at home in many fields of thought, including history, philosophy, psychology, and art, in addition to theology. In this regard, he is typical of German scholarship at its best. Among his published works, *The Courage to Be* demonstrates his appeal, reaching a secular and nonacademic audience. During his teaching career, he occupied a strange position in theology. In Europe, he was perceived as a liberal theologian in opposition to Brunner and Barth. He sometimes referred humorously to himself as the "last liberal." However, when he came to America, he was considered a representative of neo-orthodoxy. He frequently claimed to stand on the boundary between liberalism and neo-orthodoxy. He joined liberals in their insistence that religion must be subjected to the scrutiny of reason. He accepted the higher criticism of the Bible and was deeply concerned to relate religion and culture. On the other hand, he aligned with neo-orthodoxy in his insistence that the final criterion of revelation is the picture of "Jesus as the Christ" that we find in the Bible. Nevertheless, he combined faith in the finality of revelation in Christ with a sympathetic appreciation of revelation in other religions. Like Schleiermacher, he agreed with the concept of "many Christs," meaning, specifically, the possibility of the replication of the phenomenon of Jesus in many cultures and religions. Over time, Tillich developed a theological system that defies categorization.

Central to Tillich's system is what he called the "principle of correlation," in which theology takes Christian symbols like "the cross," "the Christ," and "God," and uses them to answer existential questions. Taking these concepts as symbols only, he applied them to the unavoidable task of every theologian, which is to relate the biblical message to the contemporary situation. Tillich insisted that individuals cannot process answers to questions they are not asking. Therefore, if modern individuals are to understand the revelation of Christ, there must be a preparation that enables them to comprehend revelation, a correlation between the thoughts and problems of modernity and the answers given by religious faith. It is the task of theology to demonstrate this correlation. In other words, Christian theology must speak the language of the culture in which it finds itself. Hence, each section of Tillich's *Systematic Theology* begins with an analysis of a particular problem in terms of philosophy. After probing the problem and clarifying its relation to human existence, Tillich shows how the Christian revelation provides an answer. The answer is always symbolic and even paradoxical, but it is ultimately more satisfying than any alternative.

Unlike Barth, who viewed human religiosity as idolatrous, Tillich saw religion in a more positive light, as the primary way in which humans cultivate practice and reflect on the predicament of their existence. Tillich was also more philosophically oriented than Barth was, appreciating philosophical and theological discourse as a human means of searching for meaning. His task was to correlate the answers provided by the Christian tradition with the questions people were asking. An admirer of Kierkegaard but also of nontheistic existentialists such as Nietzsche, he thought existentialists were asking the questions of meaning in the most important way. What he appreciated most about existentialist thought was that it starts not with abstract thought and reflection but rather with passionate engagement and intuition to explore the meaning of human existence.

We can think of existentialism's influence on Tillich in at least two ways. First, Tillich thought of faith as "ultimate concern," that is, as the state of being grasped by something ultimate, holy, and absolute. At first, this sounds like Barth, since the individual is being grasped by the divine. However, by calling it a "concern," Tillich also signals that human beings are naturally oriented to the divine, even if, as sinners, we are often mistaken about what is ultimate. Thus, like Barth, Tillich affirms that humans are idolatrous, in that they tend to give their ultimate allegiance to penultimate things.

The second way Tillich was influenced by existentialist thought is that he used existentialist categories to claim that what concerns us ultimately is our existence or being, and the threat of nonbeing. That threat, for existentialists, describes the human predicament. Tillich calls nonbeing "estrangement," by which he means the feeling humans have of being alienated or cut off from the source of their being, which, for Tillich, is God, or what he calls "Being itself." Naturally, this predicament is manifested in different ways, depending on one's culture. For people in the West, it has been described as guilt and anxiety, or, in Tillich's time, as "meaninglessness," something he held in common with Nietzsche, who, as we saw earlier, had no answer to the human condition of nihilism. However, unlike Nietzsche's atheist philosophical existentialism, which had no answer either, Tillich saw the answer in God's revelation, found in Jesus Christ, whom Tillich called "the New Being." For Tillich, humanity is reconciled to the source of its being in Jesus Christ.

Like Barth, Tillich was suspicious of humanity's tendency toward idolatry, but unlike Barth, Tillich viewed faith as a person's ultimate concern, which has to do with being. Faith, then, directs us toward Being itself (God) as our ultimate concern. When we speak of God, according to Tillich, we must speak symbolically. The only non-symbolic statement we can conceptualize about God is Being itself, and even such terminology takes us to the realm of symbol and myth. Ultimately, the world cannot be conceived as something separate from God, for this world is the medium of God's continuing activity, an extension, so to speak, of God's Being.

Put into the context of idolatry, this means that when we consider anything other than God as absolute, whether that be family, nation, or even self, that is idolatry, for in some sense we are substituting them for God and settling for false being. However, another way to be idolatrous is to treat symbols of God as ultimate or literal truths. Hence, anything we say about God, such as calling God Father, or Mother, or speaking of God as male, personal, powerful, loving, or even thinking about God as a Trinity—all is symbolic. Similarly, when we speak of God causing certain things, this, too, is symbolic. Of course, what is significant here is that symbols are pointers, and insofar as they point to Being itself, are helpful. Nevertheless, to make symbols ultimate is to bring God to the level of human understanding, which is idolatry. For Tillich, any attempt to take penultimate things literally, that is, as ultimate and worthy of allegiance, is to domesticate God. Tillich finds that the popular idea of God as personal, sovereign, omnipotent, and so forth, is idolatrous and unworthy of our ultimate concern. Thus, Tillich startled his hearers by telling them he did not believe that "God" exists, suggesting that we dispense with the term "God" for the twenty-first century.

The Church Alumni Association

For Tillich, God dos not "exist," for existence is a quality of dependence. A god who exists is simply another being; even if we call God the Supreme Being, God is still on the same level of other beings. Hence, instead of looking outside nature for a supernatural being called God, Tillich looks through nature to its transcendent ground and depth. God, according to Tillich, is not a being but Being itself, or better yet, the "Ground of Being," the power of being that enables all existence.

While Tillich has been called "nonchristian" and even "atheistic," perhaps the best way to describe him is as mystical, for, like others we have examined, he utilized the realm of negative or apophatic theology, enveloped in what some Christian mystics called "the cloud of unknowing." As the fourteenth-century mystical theologian Meister Eckhart put it, "I pray to God to rid me of God." Tillich's God is "a God above God," always more than the personal God to whom we pray. Though God is experienced as the unconditioned in life, as the power from which life derives, God can never be an object beside other objects. In this respect, we must agree with Tillich: God is the depth of reality from which all objects draw their reality.

The God who is above theism is a paradoxical God. This, for Tillich, is the God we find at the heart of the Christian message. Only a church that remains at the foot of the cross, under the crucified Christ, is able to question itself and thus, to carry on through uncertainty and ambiguity. The cross, for Tillich, is the church's symbol, for it always points beyond religion to the God beyond God. It is at the foot of this cross that believers most fully experience God's grace.

For Tillich, the Christian claim that Christ reveals the truth includes the claim that wherever truth appears, it is harmonious with Christ. While Tillich views all religions, including Christianity, as preparatory for Christ, what they are said to offer is the preparation to comprehend the "New Being" that comes in Christ. Jesus as the Christ is a "New Being" in the sense that he portrays fully what God intends humans to be. Humans, as they exist in this world, fall short of what God creates them to be. In Jesus we find a person in complete unity with God, meeting life's temptations and misfortunes with the grace of God. Jesus is not the Christ by nature, but becomes Christ because God is present in him, in a full and revelatory manner. This does not mean that revelation ceases in the year 33, but rather that all revelation is to be tested and weighed by the revelation that comes through Christ.

Rethinking Revelation

As a religion, Christianity has no superiority over other religions: Christians are no more righteous than members of other faith traditions. Nevertheless, that to which Christianity witnesses—the Christ—is final. Christians should not set up Jesus as a heteronomous authority who demands obedience. Rather, in Jesus as the Christ we find the answer to the questions asked in other religions about the relationship of humans with the ultimate and with one another. In Christ we find—not a new law—but the true nature of existence. For Tillich, any "Jesus-centered" religion is idolatrous. He believes that liberal theology often falls into this error. It is not Jesus the man whom we worship, but the mystery of God—what Tillich calls "the Christ"—that shines through him.

Carl F. H. Henry (1913-2003)

At the opposite end of the Protestant spectrum from Tillich we find the fundamentalist theology of Carl Henry. Where Barth and Tillich bring suspicion into their faith, Henry and all other evangelical fundamentalists direct their suspicion outward, toward secular culture and liberal theology. As we might expect, fundamentalism offers a less mystical and more assured form of faith.

To understand this movement, we go back to the early 1900s, to a period when a group of evangelical Christians published a series of statements known as *The Fundamentals*, which focused on five doctrinal affirmations that they saw as essential to the Christian faith. The most important of these was the doctrine of the inerrancy of scripture, a doctrine developed in the nineteenth century by Princeton theologians such as Charles Hodge to combat the threat of liberal theology.

Evangelical theology, while outside the mainstream of Christianity, continued to thrive in the United States during the twentieth century. It saw an intellectual revival after World War II, highlighted by the publication in 1947 of Henry's *The Uneasy Conscience of Modern Fundamentalism*. Henry affirmed the infallibility of the Bible, the uniqueness of Christ's redeeming work on the cross, and the idea that God's grace is received through a personal act of conversion in which one is "born again." However, Henry was critical of the intolerant, separatist attitude of fundamentalism and argued that it had lost sight of evangelical responsibility for reforming and humanizing society.

The Church Alumni Association

Henry's career was characterized by an apologetic effort to engage modernity from the perspective of traditional evangelical Christianity, but also to offer an intellectually viable alternative to theological perspectives he believed had succumbed to the relativism of modernity. After embarking on a teaching career, in 1956 he became the editor of the evangelical magazine *Christianity Today*, a position he held for twelve years.

According to Henry, revelation is the source of all truth. Like Barth, Henry argued for an objectivist understanding of God's revelation. However, where Barth focused on Jesus Christ as the revelation, as the sole Word of God, and on the Bible as a witness to this Word, Henry argued that the words of the Bible themselves give us "fixed truths," "moral absolutes," and "a sure and final hope." Thus, unlike Barth, Henry viewed the Bible as absolute truth. The Bible, he believed, comes to humans from without, and consequently serves as an authority to which they must completely submit.

Henry also differed from Barth in that he saw the apologetic task as rational. His task, then, was to counter the arguments of those suspicious of fundamentalist Christianity, demonstrating, in philosophical terms, the rationality of the Bible and of its doctrinal teachings. He did this by adopting a philosophical approach called "presuppositionalism," arguing that all systems of thought are grounded in first principles that cannot be proved with certainty, though they can be rationally defended. His presuppositional starting point was that revelation is the source of all ultimate truth, and that the Bible is the depository of this truth.

From this starting point, Henry argued that rationality is a God-given means to an end of certainty, for it has its basis in the living God. Based on the presupposition that everything in the Bible is literally true, we can arrive at doctrinal certainty. The Bible, therefore, is not primarily metaphorical, nor is its narrative essentially story driven. Rather, it contains God's view of God, the world, and humanity. These cognitive truths had been given by revelation to entrusted spokespersons who recorded the divinely given information in scripture.

Whereas conservative Christians affirmed that God inspired the authors of the Bible in such a way that what they wrote is what God intended for humans to know, most neo-orthodox theologians disagreed, distinguishing between verbal revelation (that God speaks to humans by means of propositions or statements) and revelation through encounter (that God speaks to humans through existential, spiritual encounter that cannot be fully or even accurately conveyed in words).

Utilizing rationalistic arguments, Henry criticized Barth and others who did not treat the Bible in this verbal, propositional manner. The price Henry was willing to pay for his perspective was a denial of the Bible as literature, arguing instead for a literalist form of interpretation. There was, however, one caveat: for Henry, biblical inerrancy only holds true for the autographs, that is, for the original manuscripts of the Bible, and not for later copies. Unfortunately, later copies are all we have. However, while copies may not be inerrant, they are infallible, meaning that they cannot lead believers astray in their knowledge of God and God's will. What exactly the difference is between infallibility and inerrancy, we cannot always say, but the difference does allow some room to maneuver, for example, in conflicts between science and scripture on the origins of the world and of humanity.

In sum, what Henry wished to give us is a Bible that serves as a handbook of truth, a compendium of information literally reliable and a source of absolute certainty, a view not only at odds with mainstream Catholic and Protestant orthodoxy, but also with modern and postmodern views of revelation.

The Nature–Grace Debate

During the nineteenth and twentieth centuries, modernity came under significant scrutiny. While Protestant liberalism made major concessions, accommodating to the prevailing ethos, for some Protestant thinkers, such as Barth and Henry, and for Roman Catholic thinkers in general, modernity became not only the object of suspicion, but anathema. Not surprisingly, the perspective of official Catholic thinkers in the first half of the twentieth century, at least until the 1960s, was quite different from that of mainline Protestant thinkers. Between 1962 and 1965, Catholics met at a church council known as Vatican Two, where official Catholicism took a number of measures that signaled greater openness to the modern world and its governing principles. Nevertheless, questions of modernism have not been fully resolved in the Catholic Church.

In the decades following the first Vatican Council of 1869, antimodernist Catholics took charge by initiating the dogma of papal infallibility. In 1910, this was followed by a requirement that all Catholic clergy, including seminary professors, swear the Anti-Modernist oath, whereby church officials promised to "firmly hold and accept each and every definition of the inerrant teaching of the Church, with all she has maintained and declared, but especially those points of doctrine which expressly combat the errors of our time." By so promising, clergy and church teachers were agreeing to the following principles: (1) that the church alone was the guardian of scripture, (2) that the truth guarded and maintained by the church is unchangeable, (3) that faith is the assent of the intellect to revealed truth as mediated by the Catholic Church and not a matter of private spirituality, and (4) that God could be known and God's existence proved by natural reason.

By reaffirming that its teachings were to be based on the thought of the medieval theologian Thomas Aquinas, or more specifically, on a particular interpretation of Aquinas's thought, the Anti-Modernist Oath brings us to a major deliberation in medieval scholasticism known as the nature-grace debate. What was at stake in that debate was the relationship between philosophy and theology, better known as natural theology and revealed theology, the first representing the realm of nature and the latter the realm of grace.

In this regard, "nature" refers to that part of creation that is ordered by natural law, namely, the physical, natural world order, including human life and its institutions. "Grace" refers to transcendent, metaphysical reality, ruled by God's supernatural law. Whereas earlier, Augustine had argued that due to original sin, humans were unable to know or choose the good and therefore were completely dependent upon God's grace in matters of truth and salvation, Aquinas disagreed. Distinguishing between "natural" and "supernatural" virtues, Aquinas believed that humans could attain goodness through natural virtues such as prudence, justice, temperance, and courage. While Aquinas did not deny original sin, he believed that its effect upon the human race is not as radical as Augustine had taught. Though Adam's corrupted nature is transmitted to his descendants, mankind's rational powers are not impaired.

For Aquinas, reason and revelation were not contradictory. To attain truth, humans must begin with knowledge and reason, that is, with scientific and philosophical truths, and add to them the teachings of faith, that is, the truths of revealed theology. Thus, humans are redeemed through a twofold process, primarily through church sacraments, but also through meritorious works (that is, through personal piety and spirituality). Following Augustine, Aquinas distinguished between two forms of grace, the first cooperative (whereby humans work with God), and the second operative (given by God through the church). However, whereas for Augustine,

Rethinking Revelation

human beings are ultimately dependent upon God's grace for salvation and truth, for Aquinas, humans are motivated by both grace and works.

In the sixteenth century, Reformers such as Martin Luther and John Calvin denied such distinctions, repudiating any suggestion that people could merit God's grace. Modernist thinkers would challenge the distinction between operative and cooperative grace, disputing the claims of both reformation and medieval theologians by arguing in favor of natural theology. They maintained that human beings could live morally, discover truth, and find meaning in life through natural and scientific reason alone, apart from divine assistance.

In the twentieth century, this led to a comprehensive philosophical view espoused by Catholic thinkers known as Neo-Scholasticism, which maintained that human beings could gain true knowledge of reality—not as it appears, but as it really is—through sense perception, and that they could reason from this knowledge of the world to metaphysical reality and ultimately to God as the cause of all that is. This knowledge might be limited and imperfect knowledge of God, but it could be real knowledge. Building on the medieval idea of "the analogy of being," twentieth-century "Neo-Scholastic" Catholic thinkers believed they could establish a philosophical foundation for theology, for those truths of God, the world, and humanity that are not available exclusively through natural reason but are revealed by God through the church.

Over time, Catholic theologians such as Hans Urs von Balthasar (1905–1988), Karl Rahner (1904–1984), and Hans Küng (1928–2021) departed from this official thinking, as have multitudes of Catholic laypeople, many of whom have abandoned official church teaching and even the church itself.

Postmodern Traditionalism

In chapter 7, we introduced the thought of the Catholic philosopher Gianni Vattimo and of the Jewish philosopher Emmanuel Levinas. We find in both Vattimo and Levinas a radical vision of surrender of self, a surrender to justice that does not bring advantage to the self. As Levinas conceives it, this is the heart of Judaism, a way for tradition to work itself out in the contemporary world. He talks about the study of Torah, which he describes as "the permanent revision and updating of the content of revelation." Torah—or revelation in general—needs to be constantly studied, and through this process revised and updated. In taking this approach, Levinas was not abandoning Judaism, but remained a devout believer, richly informed by Jewish tradition.

Like some postmodern Christian thinkers, Levinas combines a postmodern critique of metaphysics with a recovery of forms of reasoning derived from premodern religious traditions. Modern philosophy had insisted on the autonomy of reason as humanity's sole intellectual authority, an autonomy questioned by postmodernism. By so doing, postmodernism opened the door to tradition and revelation as contexts for reason to do its work.

In this postmodern sense, faith can be viewed as assent to this revelation, and religious thought becomes "faith seeking understanding," which both builds on tradition while expanding its boundaries. Thus, unlike atheistic postmodernism, this application of postmodernist principles views faith as something that energizes our living, that helps us make decisions and live morally.

However, the question remains, "Can humans appeal to revelation and to God's sovereignty in such a way that frees them from slavery to tradition and to the past?"

If we follow Ricoeur, we see that this process of coming to understanding about faith also involves suspicion, critical thought, and a close and radical examination of our beliefs. Here we note a basic difference between fundamentalists like Carl Henry and nonfundamentalists like Ricoeur, Levinas, Tillich, and even Barth. As we saw, Henry understood the Bible as a depository of truth, as a compendium of propositions about God, the world, and humanity. Building on these truths, Henry believed we could then reason our way to the details of our religious lives. However, Ricoeur, Levinas, and Barth saw revelation differently. For Barth, Jesus Christ is the revelation, and the Bible is a witness to that revelation and not the revelation itself. For Ricoeur, revelation is less a command than an appeal to our imagination, and for Levinas, revelation is an appeal to turn to "the other" in love and responsibility. Despite the differences between Barth, Levinas, and Ricoeur, all agree that revelation is not something propositional, meaning that revelation requires interpretation and imagination if it is to be brought into religious life and life in general. Thus, tradition can become a resource for discerning what revelation is, and how we respond to it.

In this respect, revelation is not analogous to what modernists seek in reason, or what fundamentalists seek in the Bible, or what Neo-Scholastic Catholics seek in church doctrine. Rather, revelation is something that beckons, to which we must respond, using scripture, tradition, reason, and community as resources for faith. This process, then, is a human endeavor, which remains subject to the correction and criticism that comprise tradition. Finding meaning in life, then, combines many voices and visions, premodern, modern, and postmodern, each person providing individual inflection.

A correction to those seeking literal certainty or final truth through scripture comes through a twentieth-century epistemological notion called the "linguistic turn," the idea that language is not simply a medium for thought but is itself already an interpretative lens to a text or a way of thinking. If this is true, how can humans identify something as coming from a source that is not human? The "linguistic turn" radically historicizes human language and hence, our experience of the world. We humans are so stuck in history and tradition that it is impossible for us to distinguish in a text or in a doctrine what is divine and what is human. This explains why Barth, for example, was so tentative in speaking of revelation, avoiding at all costs its connection with anything natural or human.

Rowan Williams (born 1950), Archbishop of Canterbury from 2002 to 2012, brought together the threads of the postmodern theological discussion by acknowledging the value of the hermeneutics of suspicion, arguing that it provides interpretive frameworks that make possible incisive insights into human behavior. For Williams, suspicion in the context of faith, like doubt, is a kind of spiritual practice or spiritual therapy. Williams's approach to the question of how we know that something comes from God rather than from the human is that we don't. However, if we assume from the start that everything comes from the human, we will not be able to attend carefully enough to claims of revelation or religious experience that senses the possibility that something comes from God.

Williams's definition of revelation is simple and uncontroversial, "What has been shown to us by God's will and action." However, he acknowledges that revelation as a concept has frequently been put to corrupt use. He rejects two of the most common ways of thinking about revelation in the modern period—both the liberal and the fundamentalist. Revelation, he argues, is the grace and the forgiveness that allows us to break with the status quo, that brings creativity into our lives and nudges us to forge new patterns of connection with others and with God.

In this respect, he agrees with Barth. Revelation is something given to us, and hence, untouched by history and interpretation. However, it is not something we can possess or grasp, or even something we can use to solve debates or to verify subjective points of view. Nevertheless, Williams fears that Barth has gone too far in separating revelation from the realm of humanity. In this respect, Williams follows Ricoeur, understanding revelation as coming from beyond the human yet as enabling us to view reality in new ways, intuiting new possibilities for ourselves and our communities of faith.

Such a view leads to the following conclusions: (1) that revelation breaks existing frames of reference, pushing us to examine our religious lives critically, and (2) that revelation initiates new possibilities for life, individually and communally, enabling us to live out of the resources of what Jesus called "the kingdom of God." Our calling, then, as Christians, is to embark on the process of discovering, in history and with others, what this new world entails.

While we might thing that history and interpretation are the problem—things that get in the way of knowing God's will or revelation—Williams disagrees. Rather, history and interpretation are the means of continuing the process started in the Bible of learning what God is saying to us. This is a spiritual process, certainly, but equally a historical process. Thus the Bible, with which Christians must struggle to understand God's will, is not something final, but a beginning, a launching pad for the worshipping community. Revelation, then, is not something statically given, but rather a dynamic process of discernment, empowerment, liberation, forgiveness, and grace. This is the biblical paradigm and imperative, a foundation upon which Christians build historically and contextually.

If, as Christians believe, human beings are sinners, always falling into destructive patterns of life that have their root in securing one's life and one's community against outside threats, but also in securing one's life in autonomy from God, revelation is the grace and the forgiveness that allows us to break from these patterns. If revelation is to open up a new world for us, it must pry loose all attempts to understand it as final, definitive, and unchanging. Forgiveness allows us to turn from the past, and grace allows us to envision a new future. This leads Williams to state that revelation poses new questions instead of answering old ones. However, to accept revelation is not to keep it to oneself, but rather to extend it to others in compassion and love, to break not only private bonds but also communal and societal bonds. At this point, Williams speaks of the Holy Spirit, the generative power that keeps us going and growing.

Suspicion and revelation go hand in hand. By taking on new questions, by accepting new challenges, by questioning old beliefs and challenging the status quo, believers remain open to the Spirit, described biblically as a wind that blows where it wills (John 3:8, RSV). As postmodernism suggests, God's Spirit, revelation, and truth are best known through uncertainty, unknowing, and unpredictability. According to Williams, revelation is the call to "the unending rediscovery of Christ." Freedom in Christ is not submission to heteronomy—that is, is not slavish obedience to tradition—but is rather something made possible through submission to the new that comes from God. God's revelation begins a process by which we are invited into a new world, an invitation to which we respond in creative responsibility. However, this freedom manifested by God's grace is not one of personal privilege, but rather one that must be communicated to others, that they too might be free.

Revelation, understood not as a handbook of truth or a set of answers to intellectual questions, remains generative, a dynamic force for newness and change. Transforming individuals, it always proceeds to the community looking for renewal. Revelation, as we notice with Jesus and in the New Testament, forever shapes community. As such, revelation equally affects both poles of the divine-human encounter, as concerned to communicate God's will as to shape and reform the receiving community. In asking the question of God's nature, revelation discovers the answer to its own nature. To put it another way, the revelation of God is also the revelation of the identity of the church and of its constituents.

Revelation, then, is a call to submit, not to bondage or in servitude of what is, but in freedom to what is yet to be, especially for those who are injured or marginalized by human patterns and institutions. Revelation makes possible, indeed demands, the continual reinterpretation of tradition, by using tradition's resources to engage and reengage with the world, and come to see it in new ways. In this postmodern return to tradition, tradition is not a repository of fixed truths, or a means of combatting modernity. Rather, tradition provides processes of thinking, believing, and imagining that guide our engagement with the world.

Questions for Discussion and Reflection

1. Explain and assess the author's statement that "in order to reveal something new, the old must be displaced or removed."
2. Explain the difference between special and general revelation. While Christians traditionally embrace both concepts, they usually give

The Church Alumni Association

priority to special revelation. Why is this so? Like the relation between scripture and tradition, do you hold to two distinct but related forms of revelation, or only one? If so, which one? Explain your answer.

3. In your estimation, is revelation verbal or nonverbal? Explain your answer.

4. In your estimation, is revelation subjective or objective in nature? Explain your answer.

5. In your current religious stance on the issue of scripture and revelation, do you side with traditional Christian orthodoxy, Protestant liberalism, neo-orthodoxy, evangelical fundamentalism, or something else? Explain your answer.

6. In your current understanding of God, whose approach do you find most attractive, Barth's, Tillich's, or Henry's? Explain your answer.

7. Explain and assess the merits of the nature-grace debate. In your estimation, how do reason and revelation correlate? Are both necessary in attaining truth, or are they contradictory? Explain your answer.

8. Explain and assess Rowan Williams's concept of revelation.

9

Incarnational Theology

The Embodiment of Love

THE STORY IS TOLD of a conservatively oriented Christian parent who returned one day from the experientially based church he and his family were attending to complain aloud that he was tired of the one-dimensional preaching in his church.

"All they talk about is love," he declared, "and I'm tired of hearing it. I want something more solid theologically, teaching more rooted in biblical and church doctrine."

Of course, by so saying, he was disputing much of Christian teaching, including that of Jesus, Paul, and other foundational figures of the Christian tradition, who argued that all theology and morality is grounded in that one concept—love. Perhaps Paul put it best when he wrote, "faith, hope, and love abide . . . and the greatest of these is love" (1 Cor 13:13).

While some people consider Christian worship to be soft, fuzzy, and accommodating, others criticize Christians for their double standards, a hypocrisy based on teaching love while treating outsiders prejudicially, as inferior, morally sinful, and under divine condemnation. In the past, devout Christians were rarely subtle, for they made it clear they embraced the rigid standards of a wrathful God. How people view God is vital, because it serves as a lens through which they view life, the cosmos, others, and themselves. As one's view of self provides a microcosm of reality, so one's view of God serves as a macrocosm of that reality. If one's view of God is positive—such as lover or friend—then the universe seems benevolent, others are valued, and the self is considered good. However, if one's view of God is negative—such as angry antagonist or vindictive judge—then the universe seems harsh, others are devalued, and the self is considered evil or sinful. In light of these contradictory approaches, what does Christianity teach about God's standards, and what kind of God do Christians worship?

The Trajectory of Incarnation

Despite the significance to Christianity of the doctrine of resurrection, a belief that marks both the climax of the Jesus story and made possible the birth of the church, resurrection is not Christianity's most significant teaching. More determinative to the Christian perspective, more decisive to its message, is incarnation. Christianity's true and unique storyline has always been incarnation.

While most Christians today think of incarnation in singular terms, as a reference to the birth of Jesus, in its fullest meaning, this doctrine teaches Christians to view all reality—the spiritual and the natural, the immaterial and the physical—as one. These have always been one, ever since the Big Bang took place some 13.7 billion years ago.

Incarnation did not just happen when Jesus was born, although that is when we became aware of the human incarnation of God (the Christ) in Jesus. It seemingly took until two thousand years ago for humanity to be ready for what the Jewish philosopher Martin Buber (1878–1965) called an I-Thou relationship with God. However, matter and spirit had been one since "the beginning," when God first became manifested as creation.

What was personified in the body of Jesus was a manifestation of this universal truth: matter is, and has always been, this hiding place for Spirit, forever offering itself to be discovered anew. Perhaps this is what Jesus meant when he said, "I am the door" (John 10:7). This is what medieval Franciscan scholar John Duns Scotus (1266–1308) meant when he said that Christ was not Plan B; God did not plan to remain absent until Adam and Eve ate from the Tree of Knowledge, or until the coming of Jesus for our salvation. Rather, Christ was Plan A from the beginning, the first idea in the mind of God, as it were (John 1:1–4). In the beginning, God, the formless, eternal, and timeless One essentially said, "I am going to manifest who I am in what humans will call physicality, materiality, or the universe."

If this is true, it means that everything we have ever seen with our physical eyes is the mystery of incarnation. The Christian word for that is

Incarnational Theology

"the Christ," which comes from the Jewish word Messiah or Anointed One, a reference to the One who would come to reveal what God is doing, everywhere and all the time. For Christians, "the Christ" became manifested in Jesus of Nazareth, a view biblical scholars call "the scandal of particularity."

In this respect, Christians come to see the mystery of incarnation in one concrete moment. Therein is its strength. However, that is not the whole truth of incarnation. What most Christians miss when they fall in love with the vulnerable newborn babe at Christmas is that what is true in one particular place is true universally, meaning that what is true for the particular ends up being true everywhere.

Christians must move beyond a merely sentimental understanding of Christmas, with its particularist application of Jesus' birth and death as the sole means of salvation, to an adult and communal appreciation of the message of the incarnation of God in Christ. Redemption (salvation) is a necessary part of incarnation, already present in Jesus' birth, because in that birth God was telling humanity that it is good to be human, for God is on the side of humanity, fully like us, yet fully unlike us.

The celebration of Christmas is not merely a sentimental remembrance of the birth of a child. It is much more a celebration of the rebirth of history. According to the apostle Paul, creation is forever pregnant with new birth, always waiting for the participation of humanity with God in its renewal (Rom 8:20–23). To focus solely on the birth of a baby at Christmas is to be content with "infant Christianity."

In incarnation, God clearly wants friends and partners to image divine diversity. God, it seems, want mature religion and a thoughtful, free response from human beings. In incarnation, God beckons us to partnership, and as it happens, we eventually become the God that we love.

The Third Incarnation of God

When ordinary people become Christians, that is, "little Christ's," they embody or enact in their lives the "third incarnation" of God, or the "Second Coming" of Christ.[1] Let me explain what I mean. The first incarnation is the moment described in Genesis 1 as "the first day," when God became the Universal Christ, joining in unity with the physical universe and becoming the light inside of everything. This is described in Genesis 1:3–4 by the

---

1. The concept of three incarnations, exemplified in what Richard Rohr calls an incarnational worldview, is articulated in his book *Universal Christ*, 12–21.

statement, "Then God said, 'Let there be light'; and there was light ... and God separated the light from the darkness." This teaching is affirmed in the prologue of John's Gospel, by the relationship between God and Christ (the Word/Logos): "In the beginning was the Word, and the Word was with God, and the Word was God ... in him was life, and the life was the light of all people. The light shines in the darkness, and the darkness did not overcome it" (John 1:1, 4–5). The first incarnation—what we might call the Universal Christ—is the divine presence pervading creation since the beginning. What scientists call the Big Bang is the scientific name for that event, and "Christ" is its theological name. From this perspective, wherever the material and the spiritual coincide, we have the Christ.

The second incarnation of God and the "first coming" of Christ represent what Christians believe about the historical incarnation we call Jesus. Let us be clear: Christ is not Jesus' last name. The word Christ is a title, meaning Anointed One. When Christians speak of Jesus Christ, they include the entire sweep of the meaning of the Christ, which includes all the divine activity since the beginning of time (see Rom 1:20; Heb 1:3; Col 3:11). Of this activity, Jesus is the visible map, the one who brings this eternal message home personally.

The third incarnation of God (the "Second Coming of Christ") occurs whenever true discipleship occurs, when Jesus Christ is born in us. This stunning possibility should not come as a shock, for we sing its truth every Christmas. Phillips Brooks spoke of this reality in the lyrics to the carol, O Little Town of Bethlehem:

> O holy Child of Bethlehem, Descend to us, we pray;
> Cast out our sin and enter in, *Be born in us today*.
> We hear the Christmas angels, the great glad tidings tell;
> *O come to us, abide with us, Our Lord Emmanuel*.

Further evidence for the third incarnation appears in the Eucharist: "Eat it and know who you are," Augustine said. As any nutritionist knows, we are what we eat and drink. Christians are part of the Christ mystery. No longer alienated from God, others, or the universe—at least in principle—Christians embody cosmic belonging, oneness with Christ, the name we give to everything purposeful and harmonious in the universe. Paul affirmed this truth when he declared, "It is no longer I who live, but it is Christ who lives in me" (Gal 2:20). Exhorting believers to adopt the mind of Jesus (Phil 2:5), he also confirmed that Christians incarnate Christ, since they possess "the mind of Christ" (1 Cor 2:16). When individuals become

Jesus people—incarnations of Christ—they exchange one mindset for another, their "monkey mind" (the obsessive, noisy chattering we observe during silent meditation) for the mind of Christ.

Speaking humanistically, grace rarely means getting what we want, for God is not a permissive parent, but speaking spiritually, grace means always getting what we want, for our desires become the desires of Christ. This is likely what Paul meant when he called believers God's "new creation" (2 Cor 5:17): "If anyone is in Christ, there is a new creation: everything old has passed away; see, everything has become new." For Paul, when the minds of believers are transformed into the mind of Christ, their bodies become temples, dwelling places of God's Spirit (1 Cor 3:16–17; see Rom 12:1–2).

As we travel inward, into the interior depth of soul, we discover that each believer is a chip off the old block, a miniature word of the Word of God, a mini-incarnation of divine love. This entails allowing God's grace to heal, hold, and empower us. It means entering the unknowns of our lives, and learning to trust the darkness, for the transformative power of divine love is already there.

The Christ we await at Christmas includes our own rebirth as well as the rebirth of history and creation, what the author of the book of Revelation calls "a new heaven and a new earth" (Rev 21:1). This is the cosmic Christ Christians invoke when they say, "Come, Lord Jesus" (Rev 22:20). This understanding of incarnation makes our entire lives, and the history and life of the entire cosmos, one huge "advent." "The Christ" includes the whole sweep of creation and history joined with him, as well as each of us. This togetherness is the Universal or Cosmic Christ. To use biblical imagery, the followers of this Jesus are members of the "body of Christ," even though they are not the historical Jesus. So Christians rightly believe in "Jesus Christ," and both words are essential.

Hearing God's Voice

To follow their own paths to wholeness, many practitioners of spirituality have learned to trust in and hearken to the voice of God in their deepest Selves. Many educated and sophisticated people are not willing to submit to that inner voice, which is probably why they rely far too much on external law and ritual behavior to achieve their spiritual purposes. Intuitive truth, that inner holistic instinct, just feels too much like our own thoughts and feelings, and most of us are not willing to call this "God," even when that voice prompts us toward compassion instead of hatred, forgiveness instead of resentment, generosity instead of selfishness. But think about it. If the incarnation is true, then of course God speaks to us through our thoughts. As Joan of Arc brilliantly replied when the judge accused her of being the victim of her own imagination, "How else would God speak to me?" As evolutionary theologian Michael Dowd loves to say, God might best be seen as "Reality with a personality."[2]

Spiritual satisfactions create wholeness, and become their own reward, whereas material satisfactions, upon which our consumer culture depends, tend to become addictive, because instead of making us whole, they repeatedly remind us of how incomplete, needy, and empty we are. Surprisingly, spiritual satisfactions are often communicated to us in material and embodied ways. Embodiment is good and necessary, so we must take care not to dismiss it too quickly as "the flesh." The difference is in how we encounter these forms. If we can be satisfied to enjoy them, fleeting though they might be, they serve their purpose, for they point beyond themselves to something divine, eternal, and inexhaustible. Through God, the world around us and within us seems to be in dialogue with us. Even when our lives feel meaningless, we can still trust and be confident that Someone is talking, and also that Someone is listening when we talk. To be outside of that dialogue is probably what it means to not believe.

Discerning the voices within comes only with practice. Because we are so distracted, not only materially but also spiritually, with requirements, rituals, and obligations, we often do not hear the voice of God speaking to us, or what Abraham Lincoln called the "better angels of our nature." There is a real difference between harmless repetitive religiosity and life-changing spirituality. Unfortunately, most church religion is about affirming the status quo, a state lacking in transformative power, whereas spirituality seeks the shadow side of church, state, or culture, aspects filled with transformative power. Furthermore, spiritual gifts are best when shared and given away, especially with the needy and undeserving, for spirituality is most transformative on its way to the "other." As Richard Rohr writes, "If something comes toward you with grace and can pass through you and toward others with grace, you can trust it as the voice of God."[3] However, if we try to possess or capture any gift of grace, it enters ego quicksand, and becomes trapped, polluted, and disarmed.

2. Dowd, *Thank God for Evolution*, 118.
3. Rohr, *Universal Christ*, 88.

Incarnational Theology

The Great Exchange

The amazing truth of the gospel is not that Christ's resurrection is a one-time miracle in the life of Jesus, as many suppose, but rather that resurrection is a pattern of creation that has forever been true. Christ's resurrection, seen in the Bible as a unique revelatory event, is simply incarnation taken to its logical conclusion. Nature is constantly changing; even our bodies are changing. As we know, 98 percent of our bodies' atoms are changed every year. Resurrection is simply another word for change, which we tend to see only in the long run. In the short term, mistakenly, change looks like death. In case you missed it, Christ's resurrection is the microcosm for the whole cosmos, or the map for the journey of life. Likewise, in the Eucharist, the bread and cup (wine or grape juice) together stand for the very elements of nature, which sacramentally enjoy and communicate the incarnate Presence. Thus understood, the Eucharist becomes the touchstone for the Christian journey, a place we must revisit regularly in order to find our eternal nature and destiny. Believers are "in Christ"; as such, they are not simply humans experiencing God. Rather, "The Eucharist tells us that, in some mysterious way, we are God having a human experience!"[4]

In the story of resurrection in John's gospel, Mary Magdalene is portrayed as the first witness to Christ's resurrection. At first she supposes the man she sees is the gardener, and asks him where he has taken Jesus. However, in one of the most dramatic moments in the gospels, the man simply pronounces her name, and turning to face him, she recognizes him. Instantly, Mary sees the one before her in a different way, we might say spiritually instead of merely physically. She realizes it is Jesus, but he has become the Christ.

In reply, Jesus the Christ utters a surprising line, variously translated as "Do not touch me" or "Do not cling to me." That statement, I believe, is not one of distance or aloofness, nor is this Christ afraid of intimacy. Rather, he was saying that the Christ is untouchable in singular form because he is omnipresent in all forms. Jesus now speaks from his omnipresent and inclusive Christ role, and this incarnation of "the Christ is the radical unity between Christ and all humanity."[5] Like Mary Magdalene, where we once knew Jesus dimly and superficially, now we can know him intimately (through meditation and prayer).

---

4. Rohr, *Universal Christ*, 137.
5. Rohr, *Universal Christ*, 191.

The Church Alumni Association

In the garden at Easter, Mary experienced a sudden shift of recognition. Jesus was not simple a gardener. He was, in fact, *the* gardener. As "the" gardener, he had become every woman and every man. Perhaps this is what the great Eastern theologian Athanasius (298–373) had in mind when he proclaimed his famous dictum, "God [in Christ] became human, that we might become divine." Christ's resurrection was the Great Exchange, the guarantee that divinity can indeed reside within humanity, for humanity is forever within God.

Just as Mary became the first witness to the Omnipresent Christ, we, too, can become his witnesses. And like Mary, we usually need to start with the commonplace rituals and routines before we move to the universal experience available to all. This is no small point. If God is God, then the Divine Presence must necessarily be everywhere and universally accessible. As Richard Rohr notes, if religious leaders "don't learn how to send people on inner journeys or love journeys, the whole religious project will continue to fall apart, because we have no living witnesses of a transformed life."[6] Please notice that Mary took her journey not by grasping on to the old Jesus, but by letting him introduce her to the even larger Christ. In addition, notice that for Jesus to become Christ, he had to surpass the bounds of space and time, ethnicity, nationality, class, and gender. As we honor and participate in the beauty and diversity around us, and love what God loves, which is everyone and everything, we, too, can incarnate Christ. This is as much of Incarnation as we need to know.

The Foundational Force of Love

Pierre Teilhard de Chardin (1881–1955), the famous French Jesuit who trained as a paleontologist and geologist, made a controversial and rather unscientific statement when he argued that love is the foundational force of the universe. As he saw it, gravity, atomic bonding, planetary orbits, the cycles of nature, photosynthesis, force fields, electromagnetic fields, ecosystems, sexuality, human friendship, animal instinct, even biological evolution, all reveal a structure of increasing complexity and diversity, and yet ironically, also an energy of attraction and, at the deepest level, a movement toward unification. Whatever word scientists might use for this energy, theologically and spiritually viewed, it is quite simply love under different forms.

6. Rohr, *Universal Christ*, 193.

Incarnational Theology

Cosmic energy, the attraction of all things toward all things, is a universal flow mystics call "love." We connect to this force field whenever we are truly "in love," for at such times we move out of our individual selves to unite with another. Whenever you notice someone standing alone, marginal, silent, or in need, and move to befriend him or her, you are keeping the flow alive, spreading divine love. Love is a giving and receiving, a symbolic way of living and being by which we participate in life's divine dance.

Divine love is paradoxical. While participating in this dance often involves making a clear decision, at its heart, it is a flow of energy freely allowed and exchanged. Divine love is the model and template for unconditional human love. If you have never experienced such love—to the point of generosity, forgiveness, and sacrifice—it may be almost impossible for you to imagine, access, or even experience God's kind of love. Conversely, if you have never let God love you in the deep and subtle ways that God does, you will not know how to love another human in the deepest ways of which you are capable. Divine love is constantly creating future possibilities for the good of all concerned, and it never quits, especially when things go wrong. Divine love allows and accommodates everything in human experience, both the good and the bad, and nothing else can really do this.

The human experience of God is a reciprocal dance best described as "the divine two-step." In order for two people to dance together, not only must they move in harmony, but there are times when in order for one to step forward, the other partner must step a bit away. The withdrawal is only for a moment, and its purpose is to pull the two together—even though it doesn't feel like that in the moment. It feels like our partner is retreating. And that's how the divine two-step works. When God leads, we step back, and when we move toward God, God retreats. This pullback on God's part, described as God "hiding his face" by so many mystics and by scripture itself, creates a vacuum that God alone can fill. This is the central theme of spirituality, necessary doubt, or what the mystics call "the dark night of the soul." Such moments, when God "withdraws," feel like suffering, depression, loss, but the truth is, these are moments of gain, times to choose to believe, to love, and to trust. Such responses, we need to know, are elements of divine grace. That's how we do the divine two step: God takes the lead by withdrawing, and we respond by "unknowing" and "undoing," for it is God knowing through us, God acting through us. It is precisely this give-and-take that makes God real as a Lover. God unfolds your personhood from within through a constant increase in freedom—even freedom to fail. Love cannot happen any other way. This is why Paul declares in Galatians, "For freedom Christ has set us free" (Gal 5:1).

Remember, God loves you by becoming you, by taking your side in the inner dialogue of self-accusation and the struggle with doubt and failure. Human loves are the trial runs. Divine love is always the goal. And it begins by boldly and fully committing yourself to others in humility, generosity, and forgiveness. Loving your neighbor as yourself the first step in the divine two-step, for this is how we love God and achieve the sacred wholeness of divine incarnation.

Learning to Love: The Stages of Faith[7]

In his book, *Faith After Doubt*, theologian Brian McLaren proposes a postmodern model of faith development, in which questions and doubt are not the enemy of faith but rather a portal to a more mature and fruitful kind of faith. Based on his own journey of faith, his model correlates with my own experience. McLaren's four-stage approach best describes the faith journey for people reared in traditional forms of religion.

Like love, which progresses in stages through one's life, from the "securing" phase in childhood to the "exploring" phase in adolescence and early adulthood, to the "giving" stage in marriage and career, to the "enjoying" stage in late adulthood and retirement, faith is intended to grow and develop throughout life. Doubt, it turns out, is the passageway from one stage of faith to the next. Without doubt, there can be growth within a stage, but growth from one stage to another usually requires us to doubt the assumptions that give shape to our current stage. We will call the first period of growth Stage One, and the next period Stage Two, and so on. Each new stage, like a ring on a tree, embraces and builds upon the previous stage, while growing beyond its limits. Alternatively, each stage includes and transcends its predecessors. McLaren labels the four stages: Simplicity, Complexity, Perplexity, and Harmony (which I call Clarity).

McLaren compares these stages to the four sequential seasons of spring, summer, fall, and winter, likening Simplicity to the springlike season of spiritual awakening, Complexity to the summerlike season of spiritual strengthening, Perplexity to the autumnlike season of spiritual

---

7. The material in this segment is adapted from chapter 3 of my book, *Outgrowing Cultic Christianity*.

Incarnational Theology

surviving, and Harmony to the winterlike season of spiritual discovery.[8] Like living with nature, the point is not to stay in spring or summer forever, nor is it the point to get to (or through) winter as soon as possible, any more than the point of life is advancing from infancy to old age as soon as possible. Rather, the point is to live each stage fully, to learn well what each day and season has to teach, and to live and enjoy life in companionship with God and others through all of life's seasons. As with nature, the journey of faith is not a neat progression, and the lines between stages are certainly arbitrary. The fact is, there is no more of a clear line between stages than there is a clear line between seasons. You can have warm days in winter and snowfall in spring, and just as calendars don't tell the whole story, neither can any schema. There is no shame, pride, or regret in being at the stage of development in which we find ourselves. If there is anything to regret, I suppose it is refusing to grow when life invites us to do so, or rushing through our current stage without learning all it has to teach us.

In *Stage One* (Simplicity), which begins around the age of two, infants become increasingly independent, and it is the parents' task to teach them how to provide for their own needs and desires in appropriate ways. This stage revolves around the simple mental function of sorting nearly everything into one of two categories (things are either permitted or prohibited, others are either friend or foe, and one is either happy or sad). For that reason, in Stage One, you set out to master the mental skills of dualism, of seeing the world in twos (this or that, in or out, right or wrong).

Authorities—your parents, grandparents, teachers, political and religious leaders—are central to this stage; hence, Stage One is the stage of authority as well as the stage of dualism. As far as you are concerned, the authorities know everything, and you don't, so you feel highly dependent on them. You trust them and want to please them, and you aspire someday to be as certain and all-knowing as they are. Before long, you find out that the authorities in your life dislike or distrust other authorities, and your dualism adds a new category: us versus them. This social dualism creates a strong sense of loyalty and identity among "us." It also creates a strong sense of anxiety and even hostility about "them," the "other," the "outsider," and the "outcasts." Stage One is built on trust, because for the child, trust is an absolute necessity, a matter of survival. Simple trust, unquestioning loyalty, that's what matters in Stage One.

---

8. McLaren, *Naked Spirituality*, 26–27.

The Church Alumni Association

Stage One is the baseline of what being raised means in our culture. Here one is taught the difference between right and wrong and other basic dualisms of Stage One. While this stage works well from the age of two to twelve, many people spend their entire lives in Stage One, submitting to authorities and following all the rules. Then, when it is time for them to become authorities themselves, they demand the same submission from the next generation that they themselves gave to the previous generation. For that reason, it shouldn't be a surprise that faith and religion are a strictly Stage One phenomenon for millions, even billions, of people.

Thus far, Stage One may have felt like a school to help us learn the basic morals necessary for independence. However, at some point, it begins to feel like detention, even a prison. The only way out is doubt. We may doubt that the authorities are always right. We may doubt that all the rules are always absolute and appropriate. Add hormones, puberty, sexual curiosity, and changing brains to the mix, and Simplicity stops feeling appropriate anymore. This may happen at twelve or twenty-two or forty five, but eventually, many of us doubt our way out of Simplicity and enter Stage Two (Complexity).

If Stage One is about dualism and dependence, *Stage Two* is about pragmatism and independence. We have our own lives to live, and we have to find a way to become who we are on our own. In Stage One we were drawn to authority figures who told us what to think and do, but in Stage Two we seek out coaches who teach us how to think for ourselves and help us develop our own goals, along with out own skills to attain those goals. In Stage One, we saw life as a matter of survival, but in Stage Two we see life as a game, as a contest of competing and winning. In Stage One everything was either known or knowable, but in Stage Two, everything is learnable and doable, if only we can find the right models, mentors, and coaches, and master the right techniques, skills, and know-how.

In terms of our faith, we are no longer content merely to listen to a sermon by an authority figure; we want to learn methods of studying the Bible for ourselves. Learning and studying, thinking for ourselves and reaching our own conclusions, are part of what it means to be a good Stage Two Christian. People in Simplicity and Complexity become active consumers in the religious market. Every year, they need more sermons, books, radio and TV shows, podcasts, conferences, courses, retreats, camps, churches, and mission trips. For some people, the only faith they will ever know is either the authoritarian, dualistic faith of Stage One, or the pragmatic

Incarnational Theology

independent faith of Stage Two. However, what happens if you start to question your religious goals?

When people run into problems with Stage One or Two faith, some make a later transfer to another faith community. Other disillusioned Stage Two believers may temporarily or permanently revert to Stage One forms of faith. When Stage Two people find religious teaching or programming doesn't produce the results they expected, many sincere believers simply amp up their effort, assuming the fault is their own. But eventually their confidence cracks, doubts pour in, and their Stage Two project starts to sink. For most Stage Two believers, however, there is no going back, at least not in the long term. Having felt increasingly alienated from Stage One dualism and Stage Two pragmatism, they lose faith in both the authoritarian leaders of Simplicity and the success coaches of Complexity, whether inside or outside the church. Both types of leaders make promises they can't deliver, and neither type is honestly facing life's deeper questions and challenges.

After trying lateral transfers among two or more Stage Two faith communities, some start doubting the whole faith project. They begin to feel so stuck, trapped, and stagnant they decide to burn down the whole structure. Other people aren't so easily satisfied. Their quest for honesty and depth burns like a fire in the belly and they move into *Stage Three* (Perplexity). Life for people in Stage Three feels more than simple and more than complex; it is simultaneously perplexing and mysterious. Because this stage embraces relativism, Stage Three people feel more comfortable lurking on the fringes of a group rather than belonging squarely in its center. Even better, they might be fringe members of a number of groups, to gain a variety of viewpoints. Unable to find a community that fits their stage, many become unaffiliated "nones," walking out their questions alone. If they find community at all, it tends to be among alienated individuals like themselves.

Stage Three, even though it brings new gains, with multiple highs and thrills, often feels conflicted and heavy, like a feeling of descent and loss. Stage Two built so naturally on Stage One, and even the portal of doubt between the two was a relatively easy passage compared to Stage Three. Now, however, everything we once constructed we now deconstruct. The summits we climbed in Stage Two we now leave behind. Will anything remain, or will we end up in a state of spiritual bankruptcy?

Over time, we come to see that our grim "all is lost" assessment isn't the whole story. For example, in Stage Three, we still retain powerful and valuable treasures that we gained in Stage One. We learned, through

The Church Alumni Association

dualism, to care about whether we are doing right or wrong. We learned to tell the truth. We learned to stand for something. Now, in Stage Three, our courageous commitment to honesty in the face of great cost and loss shows how well we learned the moral lessons of Simplicity. Similarly, in Stage Three we retain powerful treasures that we gained in Stage Two. We learn to be curious and flexible. We learn that different spheres of life are like games that operate by different sets of rules, and we become fluent in the complex rules of multiple games. We learn independence, and become self-motivated learners and self-managers, adults who begin to take responsibility for our own successes and failures.

Thus, despite the feelings of loss, the lasting gains of Stages One and Two sustain us in Perplexity. In addition, Stage Three will do the same for Stage Four. The fact is, Perplexity brings some of the greatest spiritual gifts life has to offer, gifts such as humility, honesty, courage, and sensitivity, for it is the doorstep to Stage Four. Whereas Perplexity is a path of descent, it is also a path of dissent. It gives us the courage to speak our truth, even when we are threatened for doing so. That courage is not simply an intellectual matter; it is also ethical, a matter of integrity and character.

If Stage Three dissenters keep descending through Perplexity, they will encounter a moment of crisis. Will their power of critical thinking become a gift that undoes them, or will the seeing through of skeptical doubt lead them into mystical or contemplative insight? Will they see through and beyond Simplicity, Complexity, and Perplexity to a deeper narrative, a more mysterious coherence, a revolutionary Harmony that embraces and integrates all it includes, producing a way to see things whole again?

People deep in Perplexity, feeling disillusioned with naïve dualism and pragmatism, face a stark choice. Will they become cynical nihilists, seeing everything so critically that meaning, purpose, value, reverence, and wonder become increasingly distant and elusive? For some people, this cynicism is the only intellectually honest option, so they surrender to perpetual Perplexity, all dressed up in critical thinking with nowhere to go. Nevertheless, some people can't be satisfied with that choice. They become cynical of their own cynicism, skeptical of their own skepticism, critical of their own critical thinking, even doubting their doubtfulness. They begin to wonder, hope, and imagine, and they dare to believe that there is another option beyond Stage Three. To maintain momentum, to keep growing and developing, however, requires a kind of dying, a death to ego or pride, a relinquishment of our right to judge, to know, and to control. You might call this a death to privilege, superiority, or supremacy, as seekers realize that all people share in the human condition.

Stage Four (Clarity) builds on "the still more excellent way of love" described by Paul in his letter to the Corinthians (1 Cor 12:31—14:1). In this passage, Paul makes clear that nearly everything religious people strive for will eventually be embraced by something deeper. Even faith and hope don't have the last word. Only love, he says, is the more excellent way. In his masterpiece *The Brothers Karamazov*, Dostoyevsky captured this shift to Clarity when he admonished his readers to "Love all God's creation, the whole and every grain of sand in it. Love every leaf, every ray of God's light. Love the animals, love the plants, love everything. If you love everything, you will perceive the divine mystery in things. Once you perceive it, you will begin to comprehend it better every day. And you will come at last to love the whole world with an all-embracing love."

At some point, this discovery of unifying Harmony beyond disintegrating Perplexity seems very simple, almost childish, like a return home. Perhaps this is what T. S. Eliot had in mind when he wrote, "We shall not cease from exploring, and the end of our exploring will be to arrive where we started and know the place for the first time." For this reason, Clarity has been described as a second naiveté, a second simplicity or innocence best described as transcendence, a transcendence, however, that combines the best of the conservative and the best of the progressive positions, because it brings along or includes the previous stages rather than leaving them behind.

If in Stage One we know that everything is knowable, in Stage Two we know that everything is doable, and in Stage Three we know that everything is relative, in Stage Four we come to know that everything is suitable for its time (Eccl 3:11). In this stage we can finally accept that all our knowing, past and present, is partial (1 Cor 13:12). Now we finally see authority figures neither as omniscient and trustworthy (as in Stages One and Two) nor as fake or deluded (as in Stage Three), but rather as human beings like us, mortal and fallible. This awareness also allows us to find our identity in new ways in relation to others; not in Stage One dependence, nor in Stage Two independence, and not in Stage Three counterdependence, but in the more mature interdependence of nonduality. This humility before others morphs into what some call paradox—the realization that no statement about God—or even about what is true—can be final or complete.

This new realization—likened to a second Simplicity—eventually matures into a higher Complexity, and so on, in an ascending spiral of growth and discovery that continues as long as life itself. Far from feeling we have finally arrived, in Stage Four we finally begin to understand that arrival has never been the goal.

In Stage Four we discover amazing truths. For example, we discover that spirituality is about love; that knowing is loving; that we know ourselves by loving ourselves; that we know others by loving them; that we know God by loving ourselves and others. Those who reach Stage Four do not experience Certainty, however, for that is the concern of those in Stages One and Two. Stage Four people never feel they have arrived. They are not obsessed with misguided notions of certainty or supremacy—more the opposite. Committed to the faith journey, they know there is no such thing as certainty in faith. Faith, like all creativity, flourishes not in certainty but in questioning, not in security but in venturing. In Stage Four, it is trust that matters, and qualities such as peace, harmony, joy, relationships, intimacy, and unity.

Those who reach Stage Four can also look back and see love's gravitational pull all along. When they loved correctness in Stage One, the love with which they pursued correctness mattered more. When they loved effectiveness in Stage Two, the love that moved them to pursue effectiveness mattered still more. When they loved honesty and justice in Stage Three, honesty and love mattered, but the love that burned in their heart for them mattered still more. Faith was about love all along; they just didn't realize it.

Questions for Discussion and Reflection

1. Assess the merits of the statement that how people view God serves as a lens through which they view life, the cosmos, others, and themselves.
2. Do you agree with the author's view that the doctrine of incarnation should be more determinative to the Christian perspective than the doctrine of resurrection? Explain your answer.
3. In your estimation, what did the medieval theologian John Duns Scotus mean when he said that Christ was not God's Plan B?
4. Explain and assess the merits of the "third incarnation of God."
5. In today's highly charged political and social environment, how can you discern God's voice and will from among so many competing visions and voices?

Incarnational Theology

6. Explain and assess the meaning of the statement, "Christ's resurrection was the Great Exchange, the guarantee that divinity can indeed reside within humanity, for humanity is forever within God."

7. Explain and assess the significance of Teilhard de Chardin's concept of "cosmic love."

8. Assess the usefulness of the four-stage model of faith development presented in this chapter.

9. In which phase or stage of faith do you currently find yourself? Explain your answer.

10. Do you believe, with the apostle Paul, that "love is the answer" to life's challenges and perplexities, or does the word "love" sound too naïve, simplistic, or sentimental? Explain your answer.

10

"Healthy" Religion and "Junk" Religion

THE PHENOMENON OF RELIGION has been pervasive throughout the history of humanity and continues to be central to most cultures of the world. The role of religion in the current clash between cultures, whether viewed through a secular, traditional, or fundamentalist lens, is enormous, and any headway we are able to make in the future in terms of peace and international cooperation will involve moral principles that value and encourage ecumenical understanding and inter-religious dialogue.

The role of religion, whether in formulating a worldview or in shaping a lifestyle, has until recently been considered indispensable. Religion is one of several systems devised by humans to provide guidance and meaning to the whole order of existence. The original role of religion was not divisive but holistic. It was not about creating polarities, institutions, hierarchies, or doctrines. Rather, the original role of religion was to promote harmonious spirituality.

In his 1962 book, *The Meaning and End of Religion*, Harvard professor of comparative religion Wilfred Cantwell Smith noted the difference in meaning of the contemporary concept of "religion," a relatively recent invention in European history, and the original meaning of the term. Christian writers began using the term "religion" during the seventeenth century to signify a system of ideas or beliefs about God. But that is not the original meaning of the word religion or of its Latin root *religio*. Unlike religion as a system of belief, *religio* signified the awe that human beings felt in the presence of the unknown. It included a response to a subjective experience, an attitude of trust and reverence toward the divine or toward nature. As

"Healthy" Religion and "Junk" Religion

something within one's heart, *religio* involved a path of wonder through the wilderness of change and uncertainty.

For Smith, what is ending and what needs to end is the modern Western understanding of religion, not its original subjective, intuitive, passionate dimension. What we have seen in recent times, not only in the West but also globally, is a turning from religion and a return to *religio*, only it is being called "spirituality," since no other English term conveys the new religious sensibility. The awakening taking place today is not an evangelical revival; nor is it a returning to the faith of our ancestors. Instead, according to American church historian Diana Bass, "it is a Great Returning to ancient understandings of the human quest for the divine . . . *Religio* is never satisfied with old answers, codified dogmas, institutionalized practices, or invested power. *Religio* invites every generation to experience God—to return to the basic questions of believing, behaving, and belonging—and explore each anew with an open heart."[1]

Taking three concepts—believing, behaving, and belonging—in the order of their centrality and importance to institutional religion, Bass offers an alternative, which she calls "the Great Reversal." For the last few centuries, Western Christianity ordered faith in a certain way. Catholics and Protestants taught that belief came first, behavior (ethics) came next, and finally belonging resulted, depending on how one affirmed the first two categories. Churches turned this pattern into rituals of catechism, character formation, and confirmation.

However, it was not always this way. The pattern found in early Christianity, certainly in the first Christian records, indicates that long ago, before the church councils of the first half millennium and before Christianity split into competing families of faith, each defending itself against the other, faith was a matter of community first, practices second, and belief third. Our immediate ancestors reversed the order, and it is up to us to restore the original order: belonging, behaving, and believing.

According to Bass, "Christianity of the Great Returning is the oldest-time religion—reclaiming a faith where belief is not quite the same thing as an answer, where behavior is not following a list of dos and don'ts, and where belonging to Christian community is less like joining an exclusive club and more of a relationship with God and others."[2] Relational community, intentional practice, and experiential belief are forming a new vision

---

1. Bass, *Christianity After Religion*, 99.
2. Bass, *Christianity After Religion*, 99.

for what it means to be Christian in the twenty-first century, a pattern of spiritual awakening that is growing around the world. We belong to God and to one another, connected to all in a web of relationships, and there we find our truest selves. At their inception, world religions were healthy, wholesome, and beneficial. Over time, particularly as religions became institutionalized, that changed, so much so that we need to distinguish between "healthy" religion and "junk" religion. Healthy religion provides a foundational sense of awe. It re-enchants an otherwise empty universe. It encourages reverence toward all things, enabling people of faith to see the reflection of the divine image in the human, the animal, and the entire natural world, which now become enchanted, that is, inherently supernatural. When humans are fully alert in spirit, mind, and body, their identity transcends their imagination, and they can accomplish more than they suppose. Moments of awareness occur as a dawning of meaning, when the familiar suddenly becomes infused with new insight and possibilities, and when unfamiliar ideas challenge and pervade our consciousness. Such occasions feel like personal discoveries.

Instead of providing awe, reconnection, and awakening, junk religion—on both the left and the right of the religious spectrum—leads to sectarianism, ideological divisiveness, emotionalism, and even social and political hysteria. Similar to junk food because it only satisfies enough to gratify momentary desires, junk religion does not truly feed the intellect or the heart. Junk religion is usually characterized by dependence on the past, often leading to fear of the present as well as of the future. However, when religion leads us to encounter the divine, we are empowered to embrace not only the present but also the future without anxiety or fear. There is no fear of the present because it is viewed as full of potential. There is no fear of the future because a loving God is in charge. In addition, there is no fear of the past because the past has been healed and forgiven.

In authentic religion, people do not use theology to avoid reality or to fabricate a private, self-serving reality. Authentic believers let God lead them into the fullness of Reality—not into delusions, distrust, or conspiracy thinking, and not away from dilemmas, paradoxes, and uncertainties, but directly into the throes of their humanity. Unless religion leads us on a path to both depth and honesty, much religion is actually quite dangerous to the soul and to society. In fact, "fast-food religion" and the so-called prosperity gospel are some of the best ways to avoid God—while talking about religion almost nonstop.

"Healthy" Religion and "Junk" Religion

An exclusively spiritual religion is an oxymoron; there is no such thing. Spiritually, rightly understood, affects all of life. As such, it has political, economic, and social consequences. To affirm business as usual, to refuse to judge the status quo, is to support it. Jesus himself strongly disproved of private spirituality, challenging his disciples to "take up their cross" and follow him. This meant not only forsaking personal priorities but living according to countercultural standards.

What we need at this time is a Jesus who is historical, relevant for real life, physical and concrete, as we are, not a Jesus who is distant and otherworldly. We need a Jesus whose life saves even more than his death, a Jesus we can practically imitate, who sets the bar, not for what is fully divine, but for what is fully human. A contemplative way of knowing allows us to comprehend a cosmic notion of Christ and a nontribal notion of Jesus. For only these notions are big enough to hold all creation together, even all religious and cultures together, in one harmonious unity.

We need at this time a great reversal in worship, abandoning worship as a means of escaping this world, and seeing incarnation all around us, evidence of heaven come down. The Great Reversal of which we speak is the Great Returning of Christianity toward what Jesus preached: a beloved and belonging community, a way of life practiced in the world, and a profound trust in God that eagerly affirms God's present reign of mercy and justice.

Whatever reconstruction we need to undergo individually and as a society cannot be based on fear or on reaction, however. It must be based on a positive and fully human experience of God as a loving Presence. Healthy religion is ready to let God be God, and to embrace a future we do not yet understand—and no longer need to understand.

The Basis of Worship

Now that you have additional perspective regarding the sources of religious authority, what are you going to do with your newfound insights? More importantly, how will you change your priorities, your habits, and your lifestyle? Will you remain in your stage of Simplicity, Complexity, or Perplexity, or will you move on to the next phase of your faith, a stage called Harmony or Clarity? If you find talk about faith development confusing, the concluding words of this book may be the most important, for they should leave you somehow incomplete, wanting more. As you may have discovered already in your faith journey, questions are more important than answers, for when you start asking the right questions, they, and not the answers, will provide ongoing momentum.

If you are able to move forward in faith and grow spiritually, be aware that the deconstructive task will continue. However, deconstruction is not the goal, but rather reconstruction, as you decide the role scripture, tradition, reason, and experience will play in your life. As you read scripture, do so with Stage Four eyes, mind, and heart. And if you attend church, do so with Stage Four faith. As you continue your faith journey, trust reason and experience, but not so that you remain locked in skepticism and solipsism. Live courageously, and don't be afraid to take risks with your faith, not to the point of loss, however, but to the point of gain. To paraphrase Albert Einstein, reason without faith is lame, and faith without reason in blind. Belief (construction) needs deconstruction (examination, curiosity, and criticism), but deconstruction requires reconstruction, a goal this book is intended to facilitate.

Einstein once said, "The most beautiful thing we can experience is the mysterious." Note that he did not speak of reason, knowledge, truth, or even of happiness as the goal of life, but rather the experience of wonder. If, as the scriptures affirm, the culmination of the creative process is Sabbath rest, and if, as the monotheistic creeds emphasize, the chief end and goal of human life is to glorify God, then there is no better way to do so than to love all of God's creation, for in so doing, we will perceive the divine mystery. That sense of wonder, the Scottish philosopher Thomas Carlyle declared, is the basis of worship.

Walking the Wire

On the evening of June 15, 2012, 33-year-old daredevil Nik Wallenda went for a 25-minute walk, becoming the first person to walk on a tightrope 1,800 feet across Niagara Falls (Horseshoe Falls), starting on the American side. A crowd of 4,000 people watched on the American side and 125,000 on the Canadian side, in addition to millions of TV viewers. Along the way, Nik prayed aloud. When customs agents asked him for his passport, which he presented, he was asked the purpose of his trip. Nik's response was classic: "I want to inspire people around the world."

This feat was the fulfillment of a lifelong dream as well as an opportunity to honor his great grandfather, the legendary Karl Wallenda, who died after falling from a tightrope in Puerto Rico in 1978, the year before Nik

"Healthy" Religion and "Junk" Religion

was born. When Nik Wallenda walked the high wire across the Niagara Falls, he was building on a family tradition that dates back centuries. Nik represents the seventh generation of the Flying Wallendas, a traveling family circus troupe that traces its history back to 1780s Europe. "People say I'm insane," he remarks, "but they don't understand this is something I've done since I was two. It's just in my blood."

When Nik Wallenda walked the tightrope across the Horseshoe Falls on June 15, 2012, he was taking a huge risk; the conditions were treacherous, and there were no guarantees of success. But three factors were in his favor:

1. Tradition: he was backed by the wisdom and experience of generations of ancestors;
2. Safety harness: he was tethered to the wire, supported by a security system that he could count on if the unpredictable winds and the misty conditions proved to be overwhelming;
3. Balancing pole; he carried a balance beam attached by a brace to his neck to keep him grounded, focused, and stable.

Without these three, he would have been unable to cross the wire to the other side.

So it is in our lives: as we walk the tightrope of our earthly existence, we find we must leave the security and safety of the Garden of our infancy and walk the tightrope of life, heading across the gorge to the other side. And we will make it safely to our destination if by faith we keep moving, simply placing one foot in front of the other, focusing on the goal before us, and relying on three factors:

1. Our faith tradition, a two-thousand-year-old tradition of tightrope walking known as the Christian Church;
2. The person of Jesus, the pioneer of all our tightrope-walking efforts;
3. And the balance beam of scripture and worship, which keep us grounded and balanced in life.

And as we do, let us rely on the primary promise of that scripture, made by Jesus, the pioneer of walking by faith, when he assured his disciples: "I am with you always, wherever you go, and I will never leave you nor forsake you."

The Church Alumni Association

Riding the Tides

One of the great stories of human ingenuity comes from World War II, when the Italian forces were driven out of Eritrea, a country along the Red Sea. In an effort to make a major harbor unusable to the Allies, the Italians filled great barges with concrete, and then sank them across the entrance to the harbor. When the Allies took control of the region, they inherited a massive problem: finding a way to remove those barges in order to make use of the harbor.

The solution was ingenious. They sealed great empty gas tanks, the kind used by oil refineries to store fuel, and they floated them in the sea above the sunken barges. When the tide went out, they chained the floating tanks to the barges. When the tides came in, the tanks exerted their tremendous buoyancy to tug the barges free from the bay's sucking sand. Think of the power in that sequence of events. The barges were chained to the tanks, and the tanks were dependent upon the tides. The tides were pulled by the gravitational attraction of the moon, and the moon was moving in accord with the entire universe.

"There is a tide in the affairs of men, which, taken at the flood, leads on to fortune; omitted, all the voyage of their life is bound in shallows and in miseries." Shakespeare is saying that the tides not only have great power, but that they cannot be stopped or retrieved. Their lifting strength comes for a few hours and then is gone. And if we miss the flood, then we will be left "in shallows and in miseries." So there are moments in our lives when the tide is up, when opportunities for growth must be harnessed. If ideas are not cultivated as they surface, they may be gone forever. And so it is with the Spirit of God, who is described as a wind that blows where it will. There are times when the hot breath of the Spirit is all around us, when God's presence is palpable. At such times, great opportunities lie close at hand.

Examine the opportunities before you now—opportunities to be faithful, to repent, to bind up the brokenhearted, to serve. These opportunities might never rise again. Ride the tide while it is yours. The tide may mean living with ambiguity, uncertainty, and doubt; such living is a code word for faith.

"Healthy" Religion and "Junk" Religion

Questions for Discussion and Reflection

1. Explain the difference between the ancient word *religio* and the contemporary concept of religion.
2. What does Diana Bass mean by the phrase "the Great Reversal"?
3. What does Bass mean by the phrase "the Great Returning"? In your estimation, is the religious discontent in America today the beginning of the end for organized religion or the end of the beginning of a new global spirituality? Explain your answer.
4. Explain the difference between "healthy" religion and "junk" religion.
5. Explain the merits of the statement, "An exclusively spiritual religion is an oxymoron."
6. What is your takeaway from the account of Nik Wallenda "walking the wire"?
7. What is your takeaway from the account of "riding the tides"?
8. After completing this book (or class or seminar), what is the primary insight you received? (If possible, state it in one sentence.) Have any of your religious claims or beliefs changed? Has your behavior or have your priorities changed? Has the way you relate to God, to yourself, and to others changed? If so, how?

Bibliography

Armstrong, Karen. *The Case for God*. New York: Anchor, 2010.
Barth, Karl, and E. C. Hoskyns. *The Epistle to the Romans*. London: Oxford University Press, 1968.
Bass, Diana Butler. *Christianity After Religion; The End of Church and the Birth of a New Spiritual Awakening*. New York: HarperOne, 2012.
Bonhoeffer, Dietrich. *Letters & Papers from Prison*. Edited by Eberhard Bethge. Enlarged ed. New York: Touchstone, 1997.
Borg, Marcus J. *The God We Never Knew*. New York: HarperSanFrancisco, 1998.
———. *The Heart of Christianity*. New York: HarperSanFrancisco, 2004.
———. *Meeting Jesus Again for the First Time*. New York: HarperSanFrancisco, 1994.
———. *Reading the Bible Again for the First Time*. New York: HarperSanFrancisco, 2001.
———. *Speaking Christian*. New York: HarperOne, 2011.
Borg, Marcus J., and N. T. Wright. *The Meaning of Jesus: Two Visions*. New York: HarperSanFrancisco, 1999.
Buhlmann, Walbert. *The Coming of the Third Church*. Maryknoll, NY: Orbis, 1977.
Caputo, John D. "Atheism, A/theology and the Postmodern Condition." In *The Cambridge Companion to Atheism*, edited by Michael Martin, 267–83. Cambridge: Cambridge University Press, 2007.
Chestnut, Robert A. *Meeting Jesus the Christ Again: A Conservative Progressive Faith*. Eugene, OR: Wipf & Stock, 2017.
Corrigan, John, et al. *Jews, Christians, Muslims: A Comparative Introduction to Monotheistic Religions*. Upper Saddle River, NJ: Prentice Hall, 1998.
Dawkins, Richard. *The God Delusion*. Boston: Houghton Mifflin, 2006.
Delio, Ilia. *The Unbearable Wholeness of Being: God, Evolution, and the Power of Love*. Maryknoll, NY: Orbis, 2013.
Dowd, Michael. *Thank God for Evolution*. New York: Viking, 2007.
Foster, Richard J. *Celebration of Discipline: The Path to Spiritual Growth*. Rev. ed. New York: HarperSanFrancisco, 1998.
———. *Prayer: Finding the Heart's True Home*. New York: HarperSanFrancisco, 1992.
———. *Study Guide for Celebration of Discipline*. New York: Harper & Row, 1983.
Fox, Matthew. *Creation Spirituality*. New York: HarperSanFrancisco, 1991.
———. *Original Blessing*. Santa Fe, NM: Bear & Co., 1983.
Grenz, Stanley J., and Roger E. Olson. *20th-Century Theology: God & the Word in a Transitional Age*. Downers Grove, IL: InterVarsity, 1992.

Bibliography

Henry, Carl F. H. *The Uneasy Conscience of Modern Fundamentalism.* Grand Rapids, MI: Eerdmans, 2003.

Hoffecker, W. Andrew, and Gary Scott Smith. *Building a Christian World View.* 2 vols. Phillipsburg, NJ: Presbyterian and Reformed, 1986, 1988.

Keating, Thomas. *Intimacy with God: An Introduction to Centering Prayer.* New York: Crossroad, 1994.

———. *Intimacy with God.* No pages. Online: www.norumbega.net>path>iwg.

———. *Open Mind, Open Heart.* New York: Continuum, 1986.

Küng, Hans. *The Church.* New York: Sheed and Ward, 1967.

Levinas, Emmanuel. *Otherwise than Being, or, Beyond Essence.* Pittsburgh, PA: Duquesne University Press, 2002.

Lindbeck, George. *The Nature of Doctrine.* Philadelphia: Westminster, 1984.

Marsden, George W. *Fundamentalism and American Culture: The Shaping of Twentieth-Century Evangelicalism, 1870–1925.* New York: Oxford University Press, 2006.

McFague, Sallie. *The Body of God: An Ecological Theology.* Minneapolis: Augsburg Fortress, 1993.

McGrath, Alister E. *Christian Theology: An Introduction.* 5th. ed. Malden, MA: Wiley-Blackwell 2011.

McLaren, Brian. *Everything Must Change: Jesus, Global Crises, and a Revolution of Hope.* Nashville: Thomas Nelson, 2007.

———. *Faith After Doubt: Why Your Beliefs Stopped Working and What to Do About It.* New York: St. Martin's, 2021.

———. *A Generous Orthodoxy.* Grand Rapids, MI: Zondervan, 2004.

———. *Naked Spirituality: A Life with God in 12 Simple Words.* New York: HarperOne, 2011.

Plantinga, Alvin, and Nicholas Wolterstorff. *Faith and Rationality: Reason and Belief in God.* Notre Dame, IN: University of Notre Dame Press, 2004.

Reagan, Charles E., and David Stewart. *The Philosophy of Paul Ricoeur: An Anthology of His Work.* Boston: Beacon, 1978.

Ricoeur, Paul, and Lewis Seymour Mudge. *Essays on Biblical Interpretation.* London: SPCK, 1981.

Roberts, Tyler. *Skeptics and Believers: Religious Debate in the Western Intellectual Tradition.* Course Guidebook. Chantilly, VA: Teaching Company, 2009.

Rohr, Richard. *The Naked Now: Learning to See as the Mystics See.* New York: Crossroad, 2009.

———. *The Universal Christ.* New York: Convergent, 2019.

———. *What the Mystics Know.* New York: Crossroad, 2015.

Smith, Paul R. *Integral Christianity: The Spirit's Call to Evolve.* St. Paul, MN: Paragon House, 2011.

Spong, John Shelby. *A New Kind of Christianity for a New World.* New York: HarperOne, 2001.

———. *Eternal Life: A New Vision.* New York: HarperOne, 2009.

———. *Liberating the Gospels: Reading the Bible with Jewish Eyes.* San Francisco: HarperSanFrancisco, 1996.

———. *Rescuing the Bible from Fundamentalism.* New York: HarperSanFrancisco, 1991.

———. *The Sins of Scripture.* New York: HarperOne, 2006.

———. *Why Christianity Must Change or Die.* New York: HarperOne, 1999.

Bibliography

Steere, Douglas V. *Spiritual Counsel and Letters of Baron Friedrich von Hügel*. New York: Harper & Row, 1964.

Tattersall, Ian. *Becoming Human: Evolution and Human Uniqueness*. New York: Harcourt Brace and Co., 1998.

Taylor, Charles. *A Secular Age*. Cambridge, MA: Belknap Press of Harvard University Press, 2003.

Vande Kappelle, Robert P. *Beyond Belief: Faith, Science, and the Value of Unknowing*. Eugene: OR: Wipf & Stock, 2012.

———. *In the Potter's Workshop: Experiencing the Divine Presence in Everyday Life*. OR: Wipf & Stock, 2019.

———. *Iron Sharpens Iron*. Eugene: OR: Wipf & Stock, 2013.

———. *Refined by Fire: Essential Teachings in Scripture*. Eugene, OR: Wipf & Stock, 2018.

———. *Securing Life: The Enduring Message of the Bible*. Eugene, OR: Wipf & Stock, 2016.

Vattimo, Gianni. *Belief*. Stanford, CA: Stanford University Press, 1999.

Williams, Rowan. *On Christian Theology*. Oxford: Blackwell, 2003.

Wright, Robert. *The Evolution of God*. New York: Little, Brown, 2009.

Index

Abraham (patriarch), 12–14, 44, 76
apophatic, 31n3, 88, 89, 90, 104
Aquinas, Thomas, 56, 65, 66, 71, 92, 108, 109
Athanasius (bishop), 48, 122
atheism, atheist, 56, 66, 67, 78, 79, 88, 90, 101, 103, 104
  new, 90–91, 92
Augustine of Hippo, 23, 25, 55, 63–66, 92, 97, 108, 118
Awakenings, Great, 4–7, 133, 134

Bailey, Sarah Pulliam, 3
Balthasar, Hans Urs von, 109
Barmen Declaration, 96
Barth, Karl, 79, 82, 95–100, 101, 102, 105, 106, 107, 110, 111
Bass, Diana, 6, 8–9, 133
beliefs, believing, ix, x, 25, 57, 59, 65, 71, 78, 90, 133, 136
Bethge, Eberhard, 82, 84
Bible, biblical, ix, 4, 12, 26, 33, 59, 74, 86, 101, 109, 112, 136, 137
  as fallible, 99
  and history, 74
  as inerrant, 105, 107
  as infallible, 107, 110
  interpretation of, 6, 47–51, 53, 58, 70, 74
  literal reading of, 20, 107
  as literature, 50, 51, 107
  as revelation, 41, 79, 99
  role of, 99
  as sacred, 44
  as source of authority, 41, 43–50, 54–55, 74
  and tradition, 43–44, 45, 54
  as witness to revelation, 99, 106, 110
Bonhoeffer, Dietrich, 82n2, 82–87
Brooks, Phillips, 118
Brunner, Emil, 96, 101
Buber, Martin, 29, 106
Buechner, Frederick, 29
Bultmann, Rudolph, 79, 82
Burge, Ryan, 3
Bush, George W., 8

Calvin, John, 49, 109
canon, canonical, 41, 44–48
Caputo, John, 88
Carlyle, Thomas, 136
Carter, Jimmy, 69
Centering Prayer, 37–40
Christendom, 6, 63, 70
Christian life, ix–x, 32–33, 43
Christianity, 24, 30, 31, 55, 56, 64, 73, 104, 105, 133
  and culture, 100, 101
  development of, 63
  institutionalized, 97
  religionless, 82–87
church, 48, 49, 50, 53, 70, 72, 82, 108, 113, 137
  alumni association, 1–4, 8–10
  attending, ix, x, 70, 87, 136
  Confessional, 96
  declining membership, 3–4
  institutionalized, 97

Index

church (*cont.*)
    leaving, 1–2, 8–10
    mission of, 21–22
    nature of, 12–15, 64
    in New Testament, 15–19
    role in society, 64, 73, 80, 86
contemplation, 33, 34, 35, 36–40
    See also Centering Prayer
corporate personality, 12
Council of Trent, 54
Cox, Harvey, 5, 6
cross
    as symbol, 11, 17, 85, 86, 101, 105, 135

D'Arcy, Paula, 29
Dawkins, Richard, 90, 92
deism, 56
demythologization, 79
Dennett, Daniel, 90
Derrida, Jacques, 90
Descartes, René, 67, 70
dialectical theology, 96, 97
doctrine, 57
Dostoyevsky, Fyodor, 129
Dowd, Michael, 120

Eckhart, Meister, 90, 104
Einstein, Albert, 136
election, doctrine of, 13–15
Eliot, T. S., 129
Enlightenment, the, 50, 56n1, 63, 68, 69, 70, 71, 72, 74, 88
epistemology, 70
    definition of, 64
    medieval, 63–66
ethics. *See* morality
evangelical, evangelicalism, 3, 4, 5, 9, 51, 69, 71, 105, 106
existentialism, 50, 71, 76, 77, 80, 81, 82, 95, 102
experience, religious, 58, 87, 97, 100, 136
    as source of authority, 41, 42, 58–60
    and tradition, 58

faith, 5, 10, 25, 42, 56, 58, 59, 60, 65, 67, 71, 73, 76, 77, 78, 81, 87, 89, 95, 97, 98, 102, 103, 108, 110, 111, 133, 136, 138

    as discipleship, 83, 85
    language of, 80
    leap of, 77
    mature, 79
    and reason, 91, 136
    role of, 43
    salvation by, 32, 59
    as self-critical, 58
    stages of, ix, 124–30, 136
Falwell, Jerry, 69
Feuerbach, Ludwig, 98
Foster, Richard, 35
Fox, Matthew, 60
Freud, Sigmund, 78, 83, 98
fundamentalism, 51, 63, 90, 92, 96, 105, 111

Gadamer, Hans-Georg, 57
God, 28–29, 57, 65, 70, 73, 76, 85, 86, 87, 103, 104, 129, 135
    as Being itself, 103, 104
    belief in, ix
    death of, 80, 81, 83, 90
    encounter with, 96, 106
    existence of, 67, 94, 103–4
    as "Ground of Being," 104
    and history, 72–73
    immanence of, 96
    knowing, 64, 70, 95
    knowledge of, 71, 95, 97
    loving, ix, 32, 33, 40, 64
    personal experience of, 20, 27, 28–31, 71, 72
    personification of, 28–29
    presence of, 32–33, 39, 58, 138
    relationship with, ix, x, 32, 37, 76, 77, 89
    transcendence of, 92, 96, 97, 98, 100
grace, 85, 104, 107–9, 112, 119, 120

Hamid, Shadi, 4
Harnack, Adolf von, 96
Harris, Sam, 90, 92
heaven, ix, 59, 135
Hegel, G. W. F., 72–73, 74, 76, 87
Heidegger, Martin, 82, 87, 89
Henry, Carl F. H., 100, 105–7, 110
Herbert of Cherbury, Lord, 56

Index

Herder, Johann Gottfried von, 50
Herrmann, Wilhelm, 96
Hitchens, Christopher, 90
Hodge, Charles, 105
Holy Spirit. *See* Spirit, Holy
"horrible decade," the, 8–9
Hügel, Friedrich von, 26, 29–31
humanism, humanist, 58

idols, idolatry, 79, 80, 82, 92, 95, 98, 100, 103, 105
incarnational theology, 30, 31, 73, 95, 115–24, 135

Jefferson, Thomas, 57
Jesus Christ, 30, 31, 35–36, 44, 77, 116–19, 135, 137
   authority of, 57
   belief in, ix
   deity of, 57, 74
   experience of, 71
   humanity of, 96
   incarnation of, 30
   quest of historical, 57, 74, 77, 79
   salvation through, 77
   as "the New Being," 103, 104
   as Word of God, 99, 106
Justin Martyr, 55

Kant, Immanuel, 57, 68, 70–71, 73, 76
kataphatic, 31n3, 35
Keating, Thomas, 37, 39
Kidd, Sue Monk, 37
Kierkegaard, Søren, 76–77, 81, 95, 97, 98, 99, 102
Küng, Hans, 109

Levinas, Emmanuel, 89, 109–10
liberalism, liberal theology, 32, 51, 73, 95, 97, 100, 101, 105, 107, 111
Lincoln, Abraham, 120
Lindbeck, George, 57, 59
linguistic turn, 111
Locke, John, 70
love, ix, 10, 12, 15, 21, 24, 27, 32, 33, 34, 64, 77, 85, 87, 92, 110, 112, 115, 119, 122–24, 129, 130, 136
Loyola, Ignatius, 35, 36

Luther, Martin, 49, 85, 97, 109

MacIntyre, Alasdair, 57
Marcion, 47
Marx, Karl, 78, 83, 98
Mary Magdalene, 121–22
masters (hermeneutic) of suspicion, 78–79, 80, 98, 111
McGrath, Alister, 58
McLaren, Brian, 124
McLaughlin, William, 5, 6
meditation, 33, 35–36
modernism, modernity, 63, 66–67, 68–69, 81, 83, 87, 88, 91, 106, 107, 109
   definition of, 66–67, 68
morality, moral law, 3, 27, 32, 70, 76, 84, 85, 89, 133
mystic, mystical, 27, 30, 32, 104, 105, 123

neo-orthodoxy, 95, 99, 101, 106
Nietzsche, Friedrich, 11, 78, 80–82, 83, 87, 98, 102, 103
   and death of God, 80, 81
   and "gay science," 80, 81
   and nihilism, 81
   and religious "slave mentality," 80
   and "will to power," 81
nihilism, 11, 81, 103, 128
"nones," 1, 3, 9, 127

Obama, Barak, 6
original blessing, 59
original sin, 59, 108

pietism, 51, 71
Plantinga, Alvin, 57
pluralism, x, 58, 91
postmodernism, 5, 57, 63, 79, 80, 88, 89
   and reason, 57
   and religion, 87–88, 90–91
   task of, 89, 90, 91
   and tradition, 89, 109–13
   and spirituality, 76–92
prayer, 30, 31, 33–34
presuppositions, 94, 106
primal, 62

Index

Protestant, Protestantism, 32, 35, 54, 67, 69, 70, 73, 95, 98, 107, 133

Rahner, Karl, 109
rationalism, 50, 56, 67, 72
reason, rationality, 63, 68, 71, 78, 92, 109, 136
    natural, 67, 70, 108
    and religion, 57–58, 67, 90
    as source of authority, 41–42, 55–58, 66, 68, 70, 92, 101, 106
Reformation, Reformers, 6, 15, 32, 49, 53, 54, 56, 63, 66, 67, 70, 78, 109
religion, 11, 50, 67, 68, 69, 72, 77, 78, 80, 85, 86, 88, 96, 97, 98, 103, 132–36
    definition of, 132–33
    as idolatry, 102, 103
    institutionalized, 97, 134, 135
    as irrational, 67, 90
    "junk," 134
    mature, 27, 117, 134
    natural, 56n1, 67
    purification of, 79, 87
    purpose of, 27, 43
    as rational, 67, 91
    and reason, 55–58, 91, 101
    role in society, 69, 90, 132
    true, ix
religious, religiosity, 7–8, 69, 77, 82, 83, 85, 86, 87, 97, 98, 102
Renaissance, the, 50, 56, 66
resurrection, 16, 17, 31, 73, 87, 94, 99, 116, 121, 122
revelation, 26, 27, 44, 59, 65, 70, 76, 77, 79, 87, 90, 94–113
    definition of, 94, 111
    general, 79–80, 94, 96, 99
    natural, 71
    propositional, verbal, 106, 107, 110
    and reason, 54, 56, 66, 70
    special, 79, 99
    through encounter, 106
Ricoeur, Paul, 78–80, 110, 112
ritual, 20–21, 25–26, 31, 62
Robertson, Pat, 69
Rohr, Richard, 117n1, 120, 122
Roman Catholicism, 3, 8, 9, 31, 32, 35, 51, 54, 56, 68, 69, 98, 107–8, 133

romanticism, romantics, 71–72
Romero, Oscar, 80

sacrament, sacramental, 17, 20, 30, 49–50, 99, 118, 121
salvation, 6, 13, 25, 32, 59, 60, 65, 71, 77, 86, 99, 108, 116, 117
Schleiermacher, Friedrich, 72, 73, 76, 85, 97, 98, 100, 101
Scotus, John Duns, 116
scripture. *See* Bible
secular, secularization, 69, 82, 83, 87, 90, 92, 97
sin, sinner, 23, 59, 60, 65, 66, 77, 95, 97, 99, 102, 108, 112
Smith, Wilfred Cantwell, 132–33
Socrates, 92
Spirit, Holy, 18, 19, 22, 24, 26, 33, 35, 49, 51, 54, 70, 73, 112, 116, 138
    Age of the, 5, 6, 16
spiritual, spirituality, 7–8, 24, 28, 30, 36, 58, 60, 62, 63, 72, 83, 86, 108, 112, 116, 120, 130, 133, 135
Spong, John Shelby, 1, 28
Strauss, David, 74
synagogue, 14, 17, 45

Tattersall, Ian, 92
Teilhard de Chardin, Pierre, 122
Temple, William, 24
Tertullian, 55
theology, 43, 55–56, 59, 97
    and anthropology, 73, 98
    correlational, 100
    dialectical, 96
    liberation, 80, 83
    as love, 115
    natural, 66, 108, 109
    revealed, 66, 108
    secular, 82–83, 85, 87
    sources of, 43
    task of, 67, 97, 100, 101–2
Tillich, Paul, 85, 92, 101–5, 110
tradition, 113, 133, 136, 137
    in postmodernism, 109–13
    and scripture, 43–44, 45
    as source of authority, 41, 42, 53–55, 58

Index

Trinity, doctrine of, 57, 73, 103
Trump, Donald, 3, 4, 6, 69
truth, truths, 50, 59, 63, 65, 67, 68, 74, 76–77, 88, 89, 92, 104, 108, 136
    intuitive, 119–20

Underhill, Evelyn, 29–31

Vattimo, Gianni, 87–88, 109
Voltaire, 70

Wallenda, Nik, 136–37

Wellhausen, Julius, 74
Wesley, John, 58, 71
Wesleyan Quadrilateral, 41, 58
Williams, Rowan, 111–13
Wolterstorff, Nicholas, 57
wonder, 128, 136
worship, 2, 19–21, 23–40, 135, 136, 137
    definition of, 24
    as idolatry, 20, 98
    New Testament words for, 24
Wright, Robert, 60

www.ingramcontent.com/pod-product-compliance
Lightning Source LLC
Chambersburg PA
CBHW070908160426
43193CB00011B/1405